Faith in the Barrios

Faith in the Barrios

The Pentecostal Poor in Bogotá

Rebecca Pierce Bomann

LYNNE
RIENNER
PUBLISHERS

BOULDER
LONDON

Published in the United States of America in 1999 by
Lynne Rienner Publishers, Inc.
1800 30th Street, Boulder, Colorado 80301

and in the United Kingdom by
Lynne Rienner Publishers, Inc.
3 Henrietta Street, Covent Garden, London WC2E 8LU

Library of Congress Cataloging-in-Publication Data
Bomann, Rebecca Pierce, 1975–
    Faith in the barrios : the Pentecostal poor in Bogota / Rebecca
Pierce Bomann.
    Includes bibliographical references and index.
    ISBN 1-55587-827-X (hardcover : alk. paper)
    1. Pentecostal churches—Colombia—Bogotá. 2. Poor—Religious
life—Colombia—Bogotá. I. Title.
BX8762.A44B65   1999
289.9'4'0986148—dc21   98-44958
                                                  CIP

British Cataloguing in Publication Data
A Cataloguing in Publication record for this book
is available from the British Library.

Printed and bound in the United States of America

      The paper used in this publication meets the requirements
∞ of the American National Standard for Permanence of
      Paper for Printed Library Materials Z39.48-1984.

5 4 3 2 1

Dedicated to
Martha Patricia Peñaloza,
An evangelical in Bogotá, Colombia,
Who embodies all that I aim to describe here,
Who is my dear friend

Contents

Foreword

One afternoon in the mid-1980s, raucous music drew me from the dusty street of a small Nicaraguan town to an open door. It led into an assembly hall of unexpected proportions, still under construction, where several hundred people were ecstatically singing and clapping. Who were these people? "*Evangélicos,*" said a man by the door, evangelical Protestants. This encounter and others like it puzzled me. Nicaragua was in the midst of revolution and war. But the people in the hall did not seem to notice.

Most academics who study Latin America are not religious and have a difficult time understanding those who are. These handicaps limit our ability to understand a part of the world where religion is a powerful force and religious institutions are in flux. When we must take religion into account, we prefer to do so from a distant analytic vantage point: as a political phenomenon or a reflection of the alienation associated with social and economic upheaval. We seldom have much to say about the religious experience itself or the role of faith in people's everyday lives. And we always seem to be one step behind events. Liberation theology, Christian base communities, and the Christian revolutionaries of Central America caught us by surprise in the 1970s and early 1980s. By the time we began to pay attention, their significance was fading, eclipsed by the explosive growth of evangelical Protestantism across Latin America, which continues to this day.

Rebecca Pierce Bomann is herself an evangelical Christian—in addition to being a talented and determined field researcher. When she told me that she was going to spend her junior year in Colombia, I urged her to collect material for a study of the evangelical poor. (This suggestion was one of the few that Rebecca ever accepted from her college adviser). One Saturday morning not long after her arrival in Bogotá, she put a few items of clothing and a notebook in a small bag and set out for a shantytown, far from the center of the city, where she knew she would find evangelical families. The place she calls "Nuevo Progreso" is dangerous after dark, and Rebecca expected to stay the weekend. But she did not bother to take return carfare or food with her. "This way," she recalled, "I would be forced to make contacts and establish relationships."

Rebecca later moved to Nuevo Progreso and, starting with a small circle of people she met that first weekend, developed relationships with several dozen evangelical families. For months she lived as they live—subsisting on the typical barrio diet, washing her clothes by hand, suffering flea bites and intestinal parasites, chancing the violent streets, and riding into the city on jammed, tottering buses. As a fellow "believer" residing in the community, Rebecca won easy access to the evangelicals of Nuevo Progreso. She shared both their quiet kitchen conversations and their passionate worship services.

Unlike most researchers in this field, Rebecca was able to study the experience of Latin American evangelicals from within. In this book, she offers rich, intimate descriptions of their everyday lives, their beliefs, and their religious practices. She uses what she learned about these matters to answer two challenging sociological questions: Why do men and women raised in a deeply Catholic culture convert to a minority religion? How do people whose lives are already hard-pressed maintain a faith that makes extraordinary demands on their time, their energy, and their meager resources?

Rebecca knew from the beginning that the bond of shared faith that opens access also poses dilemmas for a researcher. As she later explained in answer to a question from a college audience,

> When I first went to the barrio they were very suspicious of me. I was the only North American living there. They were nice to me, but exclusive. Then I told them that I was a believer, an "evangélica," and immediately doors opened. I was invited to spend the night, to sleep in the same bed as their children. They'd be pulling gifts off the wall to give to me. But it was also difficult for me as a believer. They expected me to preach, heal the sick, lead fasting, lead worship, and visit people. But if I did, I would skew the sociological data. I had a hard time explaining to them that I couldn't do these things. Also, as believers we are expected to help each other. But if they were in a difficult economic situation, I couldn't help them, because then I couldn't study how they used their faith to survive. It would become how they used the "gringa" to survive.

These dilemmas were all the more difficult because Rebecca liked and admired the people she studied and found inspiration in their faith and capacity to survive. Yet she managed to concentrate on her task as a researcher and to find, in everyday life, the sociological underpinnings of religious behavior. She has written a compelling book.

Dennis Gilbert
Hamilton College

Acknowledgments

For all of the people who gave encouragement, guidance, and support during the two years' work on this book, I am very grateful. I am greatly indebted to Dennis Gilbert, principal adviser of the research, for consistently challenging me to go beyond conventional standards of scholarship and seeing in me academic potential that was beyond my vision. His guidance was invaluable. I am also indebted to my secondary advisers, Mitchell Stevens, for his patience with me through hours of brain-splitting theoretical analysis and his constant encouragement, and Carol Ann Drogus, for her expert guidance on religion in Latin America. I am grateful for my friends Nelima Gaonkar and Elizabeth Daly and their refreshing support through long months of work. Thanks to family members and friends who believed in this project and saw its end when I didn't, offering advice and encouragement, such as Carole Freeman, my grandmother Helen Pierce, my parents Allan and Annie Pierce, my grandfather Everet Hedahl, John and Michele Vasselli, and countless others; to Cecelia Gómez for her wisdom and guidance during the fieldwork; and to CEUCA in Bogotá for opening the door to the barrio and being a solid anchor for the entire research project. Many thanks to my husband, Andrew Bomann, who was an unfailing supporter and best friend through every stage. I am very grateful to all of you, for with your help more has been accomplished in my life than the book you hold in your hands, and of far greater value.

Without the open hearts and lives of several dozen people in a barrio on the outskirts of Bogotá, Colombia, this book never would have happened. I am so grateful for their warmth and sharing, for their friendship and trust. The eight months that I spent with them radically changed my life, and they will always be in my heart. *Dios les bendiga abundantemente hoy y siempre.*

Finally, in deepest gratitude to my First Love, without whom I do not live. You are my Source and my Goal.

Rebecca Pierce Bomann

Introduction

He wears a plain white shirt, striped tie, tired gray slacks, and black shoes that show years of hard wear yet pride from a recent shine. He paces on the podium, gesturing, leaning, pointing, and powerfully illustrating the significance of his words. From thirty years of manual labor, his build is husky and his hands callused and thick. He is poor and uneducated, but his oration carries an authoritative tone that captivates the few dozen listening believers. As he flips pages in the worn Bible, gripping the small wooden pulpit, shouting and whispering, his entire body seems to be charged with a fervor and enthusiasm that fills the room and resonates from its plain brick walls.

"Jesucristo es el Rey de Reyes y Señor de Señores!" He proclaims, lifting a fist into the air. "El diablo ya está vencido!" "AMEN!" respond the believers. "Aleluya," cries a tiny grandma with white hair pulled back into a braid. Several clap. They are seated closely on the skeletal pews, the women in simple skirts, the men in slacks with black hair carefully slicked down. Children squirm, peer at others over pew backs, startle and watch in awe as the pastor thunders across the podium, shouting into the microphone. "We are children of a King! A King whose kingdom will stand in power far after all nations and authorities have fallen. Whose greatness cannot be contained in the highest heaven of heavens. Who receives praise from all of creation. You are his child! And he desires to touch your hearts tonight in a way that your lives may be made whole, your families restored, your bodies healed, your souls filled with the joy of his presence. Blessed be his name. Who desires this touch, who desires healing? Come forward, beloved brothers and sisters, let the Lord minister to you tonight."

1

"Oh Dios, lléname," cries a young mother softly. "Llena todo mi ser con tu amor, tú eres maravilloso, amado Dios, aleluya." At the pastor's soft beckon, many file up to the front and wait in a semicircle, facing him. Believers describe their sickness, need, or difficulty, and he lays a hand on each head, praying in strong and comforting tones, seeking an anointing of the Holy Spirit over all. "You are healed, healed this very moment, restored, in the name of Jesus Christ of Nazareth," he declares to a young man. At the pastor's touch, some believers fall backward and lie limp on the floor, several tremble and cry, others stand with hands out-stretched as though to receive from heaven. The believers remaining in the pews stand, extending hands toward those in need at the front, their praying voices lifted and strained with a sense of urgency. The pastor's wife plays softly on the keyboard, eyes closed.

When all have been ministered unto, the pastor sings the first line of a slow song, and the congregation joins in, slightly off-tune. As the final notes fade, he gives a simple benediction and prayer, and the meeting has ended. Hugs, greetings, and hand-shakes are exchanged among many as families and individuals approach the door and step out into the cool evening air of the street. Above their exit is a crude hand-painted sign that faces the working-class neighborhood, reading "Hijos del Rey Iglesia Evangélica" (Children of the King Evangelical Church). The building exterior is simple, yet boldly proclaiming its purpose, much like the members who frequent it.

Background of Pentecostalism

Latin American Pentecostals, such as those described in a worship service above, have a recent but explosive history. The roots of their spirited worship style date back less than a century to a small town in the midwestern United States. On January 1, 1901, a group of stu-dents in a tiny Bible school in Topeka, Kansas, gathered to pray for an extraordinary outpouring of the Holy Spirit of God over them. In the midst of their fervent prayer, a young woman began to "speak in tongues" and felt a supernatural euphoria come over her. It spread to the other students, who all experienced the "baptism of the Holy Spirit" and its subsequent intense physical and emotional manifesta-tions. They believed that they had encountered Pentecost, the spiritu-al baptism of fire over Jesus' twelve disciples, recorded in Acts 2

(Nichol 1966:29). This "Pentecostal" experience would spread into a worldwide movement of over 500 million believers in less than a hundred years (Cox 1995:87).

The enthusiastic belief of the students in their Pentecost was scorned and ridiculed by the Protestant community of that day. It was not until five years later, on Azusa Street in Los Angeles, that a Pentecostal church and mission were founded. Thousands converted to the new faith, and their testimony of wonderful and supernatural experiences with the Holy Spirit spread like wildfire. Within a few short years, the movement had reached fifty countries around the globe (pp. 101–102). As early as 1916, the Pentecostal movement had penetrated eight countries in Latin America (Barrett 1982).

Early Pentecostals in Central and South America encountered severe opposition by the Roman Catholic Church and even by the few established Protestant denominations (Berg and Pretiz 1994). Since the Spanish conquest centuries before, the Roman Catholic Church had dominated religious life, exerting considerable influence over the affairs of government, culture, education, distribution of wealth, and way of life. Other beliefs were deemed heretical, and there was very little tolerance for those who questioned the authority or creed of the Catholic Church. Evangelical churches were often destroyed, and many believers were assaulted or killed. For decades the *evangélicos* endured heavy persecution for their faith.

Motivated in spite of the danger to evangelize and spread the "good news" to every town and individual, and feeling empowered by the presence of the Holy Spirit among them, tiny Pentecostal congregations in several countries of Latin America engaged in heavy proselytism during the 1920s and 1930s. Their spirited worship, dynamic preaching, intense religious fervor, and consistent claims to supernatural power attracted many, and the churches began to experience phenomenal growth (de Bucana 1995:156). The Assemblies of God, a Pentecostal giant, grew at an average of 23 percent per year from 1934 to 1964 (Stoll 1990:107). By 1962, the Pentecostal congregations in Brazil alone had over a million adherents (Read 1965; cf. Willems 1967:65).

As the decades passed and Latin American countries staggered from social change, dictatorships, and the forces of modernization and urbanization, Pentecostal churches continued to flourish. It seemed that the transformations occurring across the entire Latin American landscape were favorable for the evangelical movement, opening new doors to draw "unsaved souls" into their fold. They encountered less resistance from the government and surrounding culture, and expanded their influence to the media. Megachurches were appearing, and some *evangélicos* were even appearing in government positions.

Today, the total number of non-Catholic Christians in Latin America is estimated to be 60 to 80 million, which is 13 to 17 percent of the total population. A solid 75 to 80 percent of these believers are Pentecostal, demonstrating the movement's popularity among the masses. Pentecostalism has grown faster than the population growth rate in Latin America for several decades now, even doubling it (see Miller 1994:197; Coleman 1991:59). In his book *Is Latin America Turning Protestant?* (1990), Stoll predicted that over 30 percent of Latin Americans would be *evangélico* by the year 2010 (pp. 337–338).

Sociologists, religious leaders, and scholars of Latin America have puzzled over the immense attraction of the Pentecostal faith to Latin Americans, especially to the poor. Instead of growing in fiery zeal and then dying as many religious sects do, the movement defied early predictions and continues to gain hundreds of thousands of converts every year. Its strength has transformed cultural traditions and millions of believers' lives, with a potential to influence the course of all of Latin America in the coming decades.

This book is an intimate study of Pentecostalism in a working-class barrio on the outskirts of Bogotá, Colombia. It examines the way in which individuals convert to this faith and then continue in it as members of a Pentecostal church. The development of personal faith is explored as stages of a growing relationship between the convert and the divine. This devotion is expressed through strong participation in the church and in the struggles of daily life.

Since this study was carried out in an area of bitter poverty and horrible violence, the evangelical faith will be explored through the medium of this environment. Concepts of worldview and rational choice will be employed throughout the chapters, helping the reader to gain an understanding of the true strengths of the Pentecostal movement in believers' lives. Based on eight months of full-time residence and investigation in the barrio, this study is rich with qualitative data. The goal of this work is to provide an intimate view of Pentecostalism in Latin America through the interpretive eye of sociology. It is unique in that it seeks to understand the faith through the believers' own perspective.

Definition of Terms

In order to provide an accurate understanding of the worldviews and religious beliefs within the faith, many of the descriptions of the supernatural or miraculous in this study are given in the believers' own words. They will recount experiences of divine healing, power, battles with the demonic realm, speaking in tongues, communion with God, and much more. The purpose of this study is not to debate the validity of the believers' experiences, either by dismissing them as false or by defending their authenticity. However, since it would be tedious to use disclaimers for every description of the supernatural, the reader will often encounter language that may assume the reality of the text. This is because the encounters that believers describe or display are real for them, and that is what is important here.

Throughout the study, the terms *Pentecostal, believer, evangélico,* and *hermano* will be used interchangeably to identify the individuals belonging to the evangelical faith. These are terms that the believers use to describe themselves. *Pentecostal* denotes the charismatic, spirit-filled style of worship enjoyed by the participants. This includes dancing, clapping, prophecy, speaking in tongues and interpretation of tongues, being slain in the Spirit, divine healing, deliverance from demon oppression, spirit baptism, and general spontaneity and enthusiasm in the church meetings. It is important to note here that in Latin America, Pentecostal is a specific group under the category of Protestant. When speaking of Pentecostals, this term does not include all Protestants. However, when mention is made of Protestants in Latin America, it is safe to assume that the majority of this population are Pentecostals.

Evangélico or *evangelical* is the general name given to all Protestants, Pentecostals, and various other Christian sects in Latin America to contrast them with Catholic believers or non-Christians. This is a general term that excludes only Jehovah's Witnesses and Mormons. Although Catholics and Protestants are both Christian by origin, in Latin America they vehemently disagree on many doctrinal issues. The principal distinction is that evangelicals believe in becoming "born again" to receive salvation, while Catholics follow sacraments such as infant baptism, confirmation, and first communion to attain salvation. Therefore, most Latin American evangelicals view Catholics as *inconversos* (unconverted) or "unsaved," needing to repent and be born again in Jesus. In this study, Catholics and others will be referred to as *nonevangelicals,* by virtue of non-adherence to certain evangelical creeds.

Believer is the translation for the Spanish word *creyente,* which the members of the movement use to distinguish themselves from those who do not share their deep religious faith. Finally, *hermanos* means "brothers," or "brothers and sisters," because in evangelical churches in Latin America (and elsewhere) the members often refer to one another as brother or sister. Again, we are employing these terms because they are self-identifiers in this study.

The Structure of the Book

As previously established, this study intimately examines the Pentecostal faith through the perspective of the Colombian believers. Therefore, it is important to establish the validity of the data by explaining the manner of investigation and the biases of the researcher. Chapter 1 demonstrates how intimacy with the believers was achieved and maintained, and the nature of the researcher-subject relationships.

The second chapter, "The Barrio: Nuevo Progreso," is a brief history of the area of study, with a description of its sights, sounds, homes, families, community life, and religious activity. This provides context for the entire study, so that the reader can visualize the environment of poverty and danger that surrounds the Pentecostal believers and perhaps influences the nature of their faith. It also presents the general worldview of barrio residents as a contrast to later chapters, which discuss the transformed worldview of the *evangélicos*.

Chapter 3 gives a short summary of published works and studies on Latin American Pentecostalism. A discussion about existing literature reveals what elements of the faith have not yet been explored by social scientists and how this study will seek to fill those voids with new data and a fresh perspective. Following will be an illustrative exposition of the two principal concepts employed in this study, *worldview* and *rational choice*. These will guide the reader in understanding the strength of religious conversion and personal devotion explored in the remaining chapters.

The body of the study examines the progression of religious commitment: how one arrives at conversion, commits to the faith, and then strives to maintain devotion to God through daily life and participation in the church. These topics are explored in four chapters: "The Path to Conversion," "Commitment to the New Faith," "Faith Maintenance Through the Church," and "Faith Maintenance in Daily Life." Outlined with careful analysis, yet illustrated with examples from the believers' own lives, these sections draw the reader into the passions, practices, and struggles that fuel the strength and growth of the Pentecostal movement in Latin America.

The Postscript gives a short evaluation of the study and offers ideas for discussion and further research. There are many fascinating theories and avenues to explore in regard to this religious movement.

When one contrasts this against the rapidly changing landscape of Latin America, the possibilities are ever growing and always intriguing.

Faith in the Barrios is not a statistical analysis, nor does it attempt representative accuracy through extensive sampling methods. It is a detailed description of an extraordinary religious movement in the lives of several dozen believers in a single geographical community, expressing the spiritual passion of Latin American Pentecostalism from the perspective of those who belong to the faith and live it day to day. It seeks to offer insight into the movement by means of extensive qualitative data and sociological insight, that in so doing it may enrich both the reader and the greater field of knowledge.

A small, living-room sized, evangelical church high on the hill

1

The Research Context

One Monday in late August 1995, I traveled with another student from our "host" homes in downtown Bogotá to Nuevo Progreso, a poor barrio on the southern limits of the city. The bus carried us racecourse fashion down the route, as midafternoon traffic was light. A short time later, we were climbing the mountains that surround Bogotá, and the bus began to slow and grind. Thousands of sand-colored brick homes covered the hillsides around us, seeming to strain against the steep incline on which they were built. Passengers swung and hopped off, bundles in hand, until there were only a few left.

As the bus screeched and struggled up the dirt roads of Nuevo Progreso, pausing dramatically to find gears, we peered out at patch-work houses, tiny businesses, and storefront markets. Stepping into the dust clouds of the main street, we were directed to the house of Sara, a *madre comunitaria* (community mother) who cares for the children of working women. In our brief three-hour visit, we spoke with her about the demographics and history of the barrio and met several other community mothers. I was immediately charmed by the open simplicity of the women and the towering beauty of the surrounding mountains, and decided to return the following weekend.

The next Saturday morning, I packed a small bag with clothes and a notepad and headed back to Nuevo Progreso, this time alone, determined to stay until the following evening. I didn't bring any food or water, blankets for bedding, or money for my bus fare home. This way, I would be forced to make contacts and establish relationships. After wandering through the barrio for a few hours in the warm sunshine, absorbing the sights and smells, I saw a woman that I had met briefly on the previous visit. I knocked on the door of the home she entered, and greeted her—with no recollection of her name. She

9

graciously welcomed me into her home to have a cold drink and we had a wonderful visit. That was the crucial first step. By the end of the weekend, I had met five evangelical families and attended two church meetings. I was given a volunteer position teaching English to children on Saturday mornings. Lodging and meals were provided in abundance, and one family had even emptied their pockets of coins for my bus fare home. It was an auspicious start to my study.

An Ideal Place to Research

There were several attractive elements to carrying out the investigation in Nuevo Progreso. As a fieldworker, I was relieved to encounter openness and warmth in the residents. They were eager to help me find contacts and become established in the work, generously giving of their time and resources on my behalf. In addition, reflecting on the studies I had read about Latin American Pentecostalism, it seemed that the barrio was representative of those social groups and urban zones where the movement has experienced the most growth. This was evidenced through two main factors.

First, Nuevo Progreso was only eight years old when I began the investigation. The barrio's recent genesis would allow close encounters with the founding work of evangelicals. Marginalized urban barrios that have been settled for fifteen to thirty years already have established churches and social networks, public services and schools. It is likely that active *evangélico* churches have saturated the older barrios with evangelism, and a plateau of religious participation has been reached. In these cases, it is difficult to observe founding events of church planting, community proselytism, and responsive conversion.

In contrast, Nuevo Progreso was young, still in its initial stages of expansion, and it was almost a frontier for the Pentecostals in spreading the "good news" of salvation in Jesus. In this setting, I would be able to witness the development of religious faith in various stages. It would be like studying the eruption of a volcano before, during, and after the event, instead of years later. The data would be fresh and exciting.

Second, Nuevo Progreso was working class, which research has shown is the social stratum most likely to be drawn to the evangelical faith. William Thornton (1981) called this the "upper-lower class" in his work among Colombian Protestants, noting that this class "has less to lose and more to gain from religious change than any other level" (p. 100). He reasoned that religious zeal tends to decline among middle and upper social classes that have more comfortable lifestyles. On the other end of the spectrum, the extremely poor and habitually unemployed would not be attracted to the strict moral and work standards of the Pentecostal churches (p. 98). Burdick (1993) studied Pentecostalism in a working-class barrio outside of Rio de Janeiro, and the description he gives closely matches that of the barrio in this study.

The residents of Nuevo Progreso earned minimum wages in difficult jobs of manual labor and service, yet many owned their own homes, having built them by hand. The barrio had little resemblance to the destitute and forsaken shantytowns found in other parts of Bogotá's perimeter, which are ridden with disease, crime, and unemployment. Those living in Nuevo Progreso held jobs of low repute, but they did not beg. They were proud of their families and homes, and constantly struggled to maintain and improve the quality of their lives. For this reason, the Pentecostal faith, with its strong family and work values, cathartic worship, ascetic lifestyle, and strong social and material networks, appeals to those in the working class. This relationship between social stratum and religious affiliation challenged me to carefully examine the interwoven threads of barrio life and faith in the tapestry of survival and hope.

The First Phase

The initial successful visit to Nuevo Progreso was the first of several weekend trips during the first stage of my research. Still gaining contacts and without a "host family" in the barrio, however, I often didn't know where I would find my next meal or lodging.

Many times, I found myself knocking on the doors of new acquaintances' homes and asking for a bed, a mattress, or a place on the floor for that night. Grateful for whatever generosity they extended to me, the alternative being a night in the street, I learned quickly how to accommodate myself to their difficult living conditions. This included sharing small beds with children, enduring fleas and intestinal parasites, bathing from pots of cold or heated nonpotable water, and eating anything and everything set before me. Also, I began to acquire the dialect, sayings, jokes, and good manners of the barrio's subculture. All of this was part of my resolve to draw as close as I could to the residents' own experiences of daily life, to create bridges of trust with them, and to give real context to their religious faith.

On these weekend trips, I would walk around the barrio, backpack on, visiting families, attending church meetings, teaching English, and sitting in little bread shops taking field notes. Many hours were spent just *charlando* (chatting) with different families, as friendships were developed. There was clearly a dual nature to our relationships, since both sides contributed in time, energy, and resources. From my part, I taught English to their children, offered gifts of cookies and bread (a polite custom for visitors), gave away free copies of pictures I had taken, and made myself available for hours of listening and sharing. In turn, they shared with me the humble details of their lives, faith, and families, and provided food and lodging. Each was grateful to the other, and the relationships grew quickly.

After eight weeks of weekend visits, I moved in with a Catholic family in the barrio to make it my full-time residence for the remaining six months of research. I was beginning to see that the believers' religious faith played an important role every day of the week, through frequent church meetings and evangelism, home Bible studies, and personal devotion. In order to gain an accurate understanding of the evangélicos' lives and faith, I needed to share the struggles and events of everyday life, not just weekend activities.

Full-time residence involved washing clothes by hand, enduring the long and weary bus commute to town, and living through frequent water and electricity outages. En route to family visits and church meetings, I'd be whipped by the dust storms of the dirt streets or covered to my knees in thick mud. By the fifth week of research, I had over a hundred flea bites. *Bogotanos* from downtown warned me repeatedly about the life-threatening danger of residence in the barrio since I was the only North American in an area of high guerrilla population and minimal law enforcement. The diet was substandard, the violence was real, and life was definitely difficult. But it was a crucial step in my research, and a decision that would change my life.

During the first phase, to best utilize my time, I focused on developing relationships with only a few families and consistently attending four or five churches instead of expanding the field of contacts. These believers became the source of intimate information I gathered about the Pentecostal faith, as well as the foundation and key contact points for extensive interviewing in the following months.

The Second Phase

From January to May I maintained a vigorous schedule of visits, church meetings, and interviews. Using the "snowball" method, I extended my contacts to fifteen churches and over forty families. Hundreds of hours were spent listening and observing as more believers shared with me their struggles of daily life and faith in God. For a period of several weeks, I slept in a different home every night because the late hours were often the only ones when family members would be home to talk and interview. I was attending five to seven meetings every week, the majority of which lasted two to three hours. During free moments, I would catch up on field notes in a cafe or at home.

There was very little rest and free time, as an average day of research began before dawn and extended into the late hours of the night. On February 20, I wrote:

> I have found it increasingly difficult to write all that I'd like to. I have so many *compromisos* (obligations)—I need to go to a church meeting, visit a person. Visits always become longer somehow as we talk and share. I only get ahead or caught up when someone isn't home and I can move on. . . . The people are so enthused to have me in their services, in their homes, that they take offense when I don't take the time to be with them. So I do, and I walk around with so much in my head that I've seen and heard that I can't rest until I write it all. Truthfully there is not enough time to do everything. For me to write everything I see and hear, I would have to use all my sleeping hours, every night.
>
> —*Field Notes*

The difficulty in obtaining fifty recorded interviews with the evangelicals was not the task of locating potential respondents. My greatest challenge was building and maintaining a relationship with each believer that would allow for the intimate sharing of an interview. For the evangélicos, and all residents of the barrio, shared trust was very important. There was no way that I could meet individual believers, interview, thank them, and leave, all in the space of an hour or two. It was much more time-consuming.

First I'd be introduced through mutual friends, and we'd make a date for me to visit them. On the first visit, we'd get acquainted. This could last from one to four hours. Successive visits were as long as the first, involving hours of shared stories, experiences, opinions, and food. Only after three or four such visits was there enough trust to request an interview, for the believers were all initially wary of the tape recorder and of my intentions for the research. A date would be set to interview, which would often be reset several times due to sick children, an unexpected work shift, or church conflicts. Finally, the interview would be conducted, but it couldn't stop there. Now that we had built the friendship, it would be an insult to them to abandon it. The believers expected me to return every week and visit for several hours, accompany them to church, or spend the night.

The level of commitment that was desired of me from over forty families was overwhelming. In the United States, one's work obligations often take priority over friendship or family commitments. In Nuevo Progreso, the residents fully expected me to put aside my work to socialize and engage in activities not related to the research:

> I am always amazed at the number of commitments I could make to the people. I even try to stay limited and not to meet more friends because then I have to keep visiting them and maintaining the friendship. With all that the barrio would like me to do, I would never have time for my own life or my own work. Not even for sleep. I do what I can with what I have but there are uncomfortable moments when I have to say no. I still wonder how everything will turn out for the study and how I can gain the quick confidence of people who place so much value in the friendship and constant companionship of others.
>
> —*Field Notes*

Another difficulty I encountered was the polite custom of Latin Americans to offer food to guests. The Latin saying goes, "The poorer they are, the more generous they are," and those in Nuevo Progreso were no exception. In every home that I visited, I was offered food. Sometimes it was a small snack, but most often it was a plate piled high with typical barrio food—fried potatoes, fried yucca, beans, fried meat and eggs, bread, fried *plátano* (a type of banana), and very few vegetables. This was *comida pesada*, heavy food, and too much of it makes one sick. As I visited several families a day, I was often given meals such as the one described back-to-back from morning till night. One day I had three breakfasts, two lunches, and three dinners. Although I have a small appetite, I dared not reject something that was prepared with precious money and humble pride.

The care that was required to gain the residents' trust and maintain it was the inevitable cost for the amount of data I collected during the year. Although the research was intense, reaching seventy to eighty hours weekly, it was very rewarding, and I enjoyed the intimate sharing and open warmth of the people. What I regretted was not my decision to extend the field of subjects and churches, but the lack of time to gather all of the information available to me.

Biases and Advantages in the Research Position

As a "Gringa"

Most of the residents in the barrio had come into contact with North Americans at some point in their lives. In general, gringos were distantly known as wealthy, admired, and far too important to venture into a barrio such as Nuevo Progreso. To have me sitting in their home, sharing *tinto* (black coffee) with them, or sleeping in a bed with their children, was a delight and wonder for them. They were fascinated by me and had many questions to ask.

Colombians have a love-hate relationship with the United States. They emulate its styles, language, culture, and foods, but despise its strong influence over other nations. They also resent being blamed by the United States for its grave drug problem. Barrio residents considered me to be a representative for my country, wanting explanations, descriptions, and "inside" information. This was a difficulty during the first stage of every relationship because my identity dominated the topic of conversation. It would take at least a couple of hours for me to turn the focus of discussion onto their lives and to convince them that I was sincerely interested in the humble details of their daily existence.

Also, since I was a foreigner, many residents wanted to give me a superficially pleasant view of their family, work, and faith. They went to unnecessary lengths to offer me their best when I was a guest, which made me uncomfortable, because I understood the sacrifice it required. I worked hard to show the residents that I was content in whatever situation I encountered, that neither poverty nor riches impressed me, and that I was interested in them as people and not in the material quality of their lives or homes. Once beyond this barrier, friendships developed very quickly. I am amazed to think how different the data and impressions of the barrio would have been had I finished only a month or two of research, for the reality that was exposed to me later was often very different from initial appearances.

As a Believer

The second major factor in the research was the fact that I share the religious faith of my subjects. This element of my identity had very clear advantages and disadvantages. The advantages were apparent as I made initial contacts during the first few weeks of research. Believers were suspicious of me, though curious, and politely excluded me from the intimate affairs of their home and church until they knew that I was an evangélica. Then, doors were opened, food and lodging offered, friendships made, further contacts made available, and free services given. I enjoyed an immediate acceptance into the evangelical community in the barrio, for they viewed me as a "sister" in Christ, and even called me "hermana Rebecca" for the entire year.

The line between the believers and unbelievers is so significant to the evangelicals—separation of life and death, darkness and light, sin and holiness—that had I not shared their identity, I believe it would have taken me weeks or months more to gain their trust. The importance of my faith resonated throughout the year as I heard evangélicos introduce me to others, verifying my "evangelical-ness" even before they mentioned my name or my identity as a gringa. There was no need to convert me to their faith, a pressure that other nonevangelical researchers in Latin America have felt (see Flora 1976). In addition, the hermanos expressed an ease in sharing their experiences in the faith with me, since I also was a believer.

Although I have a background in Pentecostalism from my upbringing, and thus was not intimidated or confused by the euphoric and highly charged behavior of the church meetings, I had many things to learn about the Latin American expression of the Pentecostal faith. Their fervor was unlike anything I had encountered in my experience. Why did they fast so often? What did all-night vigils accomplish? Why did we stand to read the Bible? My understanding of Christian principles helped me follow along in sermons and home meetings without difficulty, but I found myself relearning the faith throughout the research as I studied the meaning it carried for the Colombian believers.

Though I tried to keep a low profile in the meetings I attended, the hermanos' perception of me as a North American evangelical was also a disadvantage. In their experience, most gringo brothers who travel to Colombia do so to preach and lead revivals. They fully expected me to lead worship, pray for others, evangelize, preach, fast, and heal the sick. It was difficult for them to understand that I couldn't preach because I needed to record the sermon for my field notes. I couldn't be a part of strengthening their faith, or I would skew the findings. Initially, I refused all offers to lead a prayer or a song, giving my lack of Spanish skills as an excuse.

Gradually, however, I noticed that a small level of participation was of great benefit to the research and didn't alter the data. It proved to the believers the authenticity of my faith in God and thus affirmed their confidence in our friendship. Whether I was there or not, meetings would continue, sermons would be given, and prayers would be offered. If I did participate, I was just one of dozens who prayed, sang, or stood up to give a testimony. I visited so many churches, and my attendance was so irregular, that it was impossible to make a visible difference in the strength or vitality of a single one. In any case, I did my best to maintain a casual role in the activities of the churches.

As a Resident

From my experience of living in the barrio, I enjoyed the advantage of having firsthand knowledge about the trials of day-to-day living and working. Although the residents laughed at my initial struggle to adjust, many told me that since I lived in Nuevo Progreso, they knew I was sincere in my desire to understand the people and to share the real life of the barrio. For example, if the water had been cut and toilets were stopped up, they didn't feel awkward allowing me to use their facility during a visit, because I had learned how to pour in rainwater and "create" a flush. The equality of living standards between us was a great factor in the comfort and honesty of the research relationship.

Although at times it was difficult to separate myself from barrio life in order to examine it objectively, I believe the immersion helped me to identify those elements that were the most challenging to daily existence. For example, the bus ride that the residents endured every day was so packed, physically draining, and treacherous, that they would begin their twelve-hour shifts of manual labor exhausted, patience worn thin. It takes much longer to boil a pot of water on a tiny gas stove, mix it with cool rainwater, and stand over a drain to bathe than it does to simply wash under a hot shower. To present oneself as clean and professional to a potential employer is a challenge when one has to walk three-quarters of a mile in six inches of sloppy mud to catch the bus. As the months passed, I gained a sincere appreciation for the tenacity and inner strength of the residents, as well as an understanding of their need for spiritual peace and emotional release.

As a Friend

One of the greatest dilemmas I encountered during the research was knowing that families were in need of food or money and not having the freedom to help them. Many times, friends that I had gained through the research would be short of food, or they would have a pressing bill for which there was no money to pay. Some affirmed their trust in God, yet still showed signs of distress with hungry children or the sudden loss of a job. It was a constant temptation for me to help them with such difficulties, since I identified with their struggle and cared for their well-being. My identity as an evangélica was also in conflict here, for believers are to help one another in any circumstance of need or crisis.

In most circumstances, I sympathized with the family and listened, without offering any kind of help. In very few instances where I was the sole person aware of a serious need, I would buy a small bag of groceries, and only twice did I offer financial help. As the research progressed, I began to accustom myself to the environment of poverty in which hardships are simply endured. Since my relationships with the residents of Nuevo Progreso were based on shared trust and not on material exchange, supplying aid in their crises was not necessary for success in the investigation. In any case, the believers never asked me to contribute, even if they desired it, so my presence played little part in the resolution of their difficulties.

There is no flawless fieldworker, for we are all human, nor is there perfect objectivity, for humans have beliefs, emotions, physical feelings, and sculpted worldviews. My humanness was very apparent in this field research, for the passion and struggle of the believers' faith and daily lives moved me, inspired me, puzzled me, and even angered me. As a resident of the barrio, all of my physical sensations and emotional states were brought into play as I experienced the frustration, discomfort, or downright pain of daily life there. I also shared in the residents' joy from simple pleasures and celebrations, and when hardships were overcome. One simply cannot have the cold objectivity of laboratory analysis with Latin American Pentecostals, for by their culture and religion they are doubly passionate. I laughed till I cried and cried till I laughed with them, and my life was transformed by the experience.

By traveling down these necessary inroads during the research, I came to understand the believers and their religious faith from an intimate perspective. In many cases, those in my study confided information to me that not even their families or church friends knew. My status as an empathetic listener from outside the area gave the believers a liberty to express satisfaction *and* discouragement in their church, personal faith, or family life during the visits. I was grateful for their openness. It gave me perspective into the whole picture of what it was to be a Pentecostal in this barrio, and not just how individuals appeared on Sunday morning.

Although my identities as a gringa, believer, resident, and friend sometimes brought obstacles into the research path, overall they proved to be advantageous for the work I set out to do. The investigation followed a natural progression, from the first weekend to the last, and though the experience was intense, it was also very rewarding. Now, as I paint a word-picture of the barrio, my hope is that the reader will be drawn into the passions and struggles of daily life of the families and individuals in the study.

The barrio as seen from a nearby hill—this was all pastureland ten years ago

2

The Barrio: Nuevo Progreso

I f there were a canticle written for modern-day Colombia, it would be a bittersweet melody of great beauty and terrible tragedy. The notes would soar in pride for the stunning natural beauty and abundant resources, for the splendid collage of skin color and culture, and for world-renowned music, dance, and literature. Elevated with joy, the words would boast of lovely roses, rich coffee beans, bottomless oil reserves, and coasts that meet two great oceans. And, oh, the passion of the Colombians would be sung, for country and family, life and love, the natural inclination to pour all of one's heart, soul, and body into the treasures of one's heart. Then the pride of the song would stumble and fall, for it is this same great passion that has poisoned the strength of Colombia, causing bloody civil upheaval, destructive corruption, and widespread destitution. One verse and then another would tell of assassination schools, of judges who must choose between injustice and death, of over a million *desplazados*— citizens displaced from their homes and towns. In tones of mourning it would recount stories of soldiers burned alive, countless innocents massacred, of lawbreakers more powerful than the government, of each man against his neighbor, of no end to *la violencia*. After a great silence, in which the heart of every Colombian is wrung and heavy, crying out for peace, there is a soft but resolute final verse of hope. The words would lift in supplication for tomorrow, for Colombians cling to hope as a plátano peel to its fruit, as the merengue dancer to his partner, as setting light on the Andes at dusk. It is with the resounding final notes of this great canticle that we approach the capital city via the eight polluted lanes of the street La Caracas.

21

Down La Caracas

The bus has not moved in over ten minutes. Rain is pouring down outside relentlessly, almost fiercely, dripping through window seams, pounding the glass panes, rising to midtire level in the flooded streets. A seated woman blows on the face of her sleeping baby, smoothing his sweat-soaked hair down with her fingers, cooling him in the stuffy heat of the packed bus. Those standing shift uncomfortably in their cramped positions, peering out through the fogged windows at the endless line of taillights in the darkness that stand motionless, waiting, wet.

Four lanes of southbound traffic in downtown Bogotá are at a standstill. Every passenger is strained and pressed by others, unable to move, for the bus is overpacked. Lively Colombian music has been blaring over the radio, as if the singer were desperately trying to distract the passengers from the agitation of the stopped traffic. Many of them have just finished a long day of manual labor, and they seem too weary to protest the delay. Finally, a woman sighs, "Ay, Dios *mío*," and then, as if in divine response, the taillights ahead flicker and the bus begins to move forward. Passengers strain, their white knuckles gripping the steel hand bars, trying to resist the jerking and lurching gearshifting of the huge vehicle. The bus picks up speed, and the radio singer sounds relieved.

An hour later, the rain has subsided and the roads are rising into the mountains that surround Bogotá. Passengers still fill the seats, but only a dozen or so remain standing. Outside, hundreds of thousands of lights against the rising mountainsides can be seen in the endless neighborhoods, or barrios, of the poor and working-class population of the city.

The bus finally turns off the paved road and up a steep slope, into the dark muddy streets of the barrio of this study. Pausing as passengers step off with their bags and purses, the bus passes dimly lit storefronts, piles of garbage, scrawny dogs, and weary laborers making their way home around the thick mud and fast-moving streams of rainwater. This is the barrio Nuevo Progreso (New Progress). It sits on the edge of the city. Beyond its furthest homes the breathtaking countryside of Colombia begins.

History

Only nine years ago, there was no Nuevo Progreso. The barrio was hundreds of acres of sloping pastureland, owned by a well-known politician. Capitalizing on the tremendous movement of Colombians from the countryside to Bogotá, the owner divided the land into thousands of tiny lots, each measuring six meters wide by twelve meters deep. He advertised extensively for the sale of the *lotes*, promising legal ownership and low prices. The trade-off? Interested buyers had to work on the land without pay on weekends and holidays for over a year, hauling rocks, digging ditches, leveling lots, and clearing what would be the main streets of the barrio. At last, the first few families moved to the open, green hillside, to settle and build Nuevo Progreso.

For the first few months, residents lived in makeshift shacks until they had enough money to start building with cement and bricks. Often an entire family would share a tiny, one-room house while they saved resources to construct a kitchen or bathroom. Water had to be hauled in buckets from a great distance until the residents illegally tapped into a nearby water source for general use. One small generator provided electricity to a few homes, but the majority of the residents had no light or power for several months. Neither was there sewage, nor any sort of transportation. Those who wished to go to the city had to walk over a mile to a bus route in another barrio, carrying bundles, small children, and building supplies.

The first residents of Nuevo Progreso were largely from the countryside, although they were already living in the capital when they heard of the new barrio. Many had experienced the decline of feasible life in the *campo* and were attracted to the megatropolis by the promise of opportunity and a fresh start. The barrio represented new hope, for it brought to them the real possibility of owning a home. Highly committed to progress and improvement, the residents united in teams and work parties to make the neighborhood livable. Pooling money for water and sewage pipes, electricity, and industrial generators, they struggled to build the new community. This was done completely independent of any government aid or political representation. Slowly, the barrio took shape.

As more families moved to Nuevo Progreso to build homes and settle down permanently, the barrio began to develop all of the businesses and services of a little town. It extended by blocks up the hill, requiring a second main street and another bus route. Residents elected their own leadership, breaking the barrio into manageable zones with committees, presidents, treasurers, and secretaries. They collected money for telephone poles, schools, parks, a Catholic church, and individual needs such as funerals or medical emergencies. Women came together to create networks of child care for working mothers. The population grew, multiplied exponentially, and continues to expand.

Present Progress

Today, Nuevo Progreso is home to over one hundred thousand residents. Gazing at the thousands of sand-colored brick homes from a nearby hill, it is difficult to imagine the barrio as slopes of pastureland. There are several schools, bakeries, house-sized "supermarkets," meat stores, produce markets, beauty salons, drugstores, metal workshops, *asaderos* (restaurants specializing in roasted chicken), construction supply vendors, bars, a real estate office, and many *"miscelanea"* stores that sell anything from school supplies to clothes. Houses are one- or two-story, built in tightly packed rows, many with clothes flapping from rope strung on the flat cement roofs.

On a typical day, buses roar up and down the main streets, taking passengers to and from downtown, stirring up dust clouds. Their ugly fumes contrast with the clean mountain air of the barrio. Uniformed children line up in front of schools and play basketball during recreation time. They sing out "Buenas!" in the small shops, the normal greeting, and spend a few coins on a sucker or cookie. Teenage boys race down the main streets on their BMX bikes, while the younger ones play soccer in a grass field, marking the goals with T-shirts or coats, shouting, laughing, fighting. A young girl in a ponytail and skirt, awkwardly supporting a toddler on one hip, shares *yogur* (yogurt) with him while their mother chooses meat in the *carnicería*. A farmer switches the rumps of a half-dozen cows, calling out a greeting to his friend, as the animals take grudging steps up the dirt street to an empty *lote* of grass.

Businesses slide open their doors, greeting buyers with the customary, *"A la orden"* (at your service). The scream of welding metal can be heard from workshops. Bakery owners fill their shelves with loaves, cookies, and croissants, selling them fresh and delicious for a small price. A man walks down the narrow streets between houses, calling out *"Pescado, fresco pescado,"* with a tub of fish in ice hoisted on his shoulder. Sometimes one can hear a sales pitch through a megaphone, as a car from another barrio will arrive with a load of vegetables, fruit, or household necessities to sell for reduced prices.

A young woman sits on a simple chair in the main street with her toddler playing nearby. Ice cream and a plastic bag of cones are in a cooler in front of her, upon which is a sign *"Conos 200 pesos."* A tiny, elderly woman is guided by her daughter down to the bus, stepping around the construction holes in the street. A stylist sweeps the dirt entrance to her salon, a shoe repairman sits shining boots in his handmade booth, a woman stands selling *arepas* over a grill for 300 pesos each, and a community mother leads a group of children to the grassy park. From every storefront blares lively music, melancholy music, traditional music, of lost love and found love.

From the break of dawn until nightfall, there is constant, busy activity with all the labors of work, home, and family. At dusk, one can often see men gathered in a bar to drink beer and play *tejo*. They toss rocks at an inclined flat of mud, aiming at three white triangles placed in the center that explode upon impact. As shops wind down the day, women or children will stop at bakeries to buy a pint-size bag of milk and rolls for their family's breakfast the next morning.

At night, houses and businesses are closed by eight or nine o'clock, and apart from barking dogs, an occasional bus, or a couple of open bars, the barrio is like a tomb. There are no streetlights and no nighttime activity. Being in the street after dark is dangerous, for thugs and killers roam freely during this time. Children are kept in, and families go to bed early. Very few leave their home after nine o'clock. Life in Nuevo Progreso begins before dawn, and by nightfall, one is usually *rendido* (exhausted).

Employment

A fair number of residents run small businesses from their own homes in the barrio, selling various products and skilled services. These are tiny, humble shops that have to make services available for what other residents can afford—very little—but often they provide subsistence for an entire family. Men work in downtown Bogotá as construction workers, vigilance officers, factory workers, bus and taxi drivers, brickmakers, or temporary manual laborers. Some have jobs in the informal market shining shoes or selling small goods or candies. Some women work in factories or small restaurants, but the majority are nannies or maids in private homes and businesses in Bogotá.

The normal daily wage at the time of my research was 5,000 to 7,000 pesos. The exchange rate then was 1,000 pesos to the dollar, which means that the monthly wage was only about $120. With the cost of public transportation and meals, take-home pay for full-time employment was often less than $100 monthly. Since it was impossible to sustain a family on one low wage, the majority of families in the barrio had two or more members engaged in full-time employment or informal work to support the home.

The residents of Nuevo Progreso are generally very committed employees, reflecting the progressive and family-oriented focus they share. Although the jobs are menial and even degrading, the alternative, which is unemployment, is unthinkable. Thousands have already gone to work by 6 A.M., and many of these do not return until late in the evening. Residents often told me with pride that the Colombian people *no se deja morir* (they don't let themselves die), that is, they seek out any means to survive and struggle on in spite of desperate circumstances. This tenacity was evident in their daily work habits.

Family Life

As elsewhere in Latin American culture, the family is the central focus for residents of Nuevo Progreso. Members of extended families live in close proximity and maintain a constant social and material network. For most residents, the extended family is their life insurance, food bank, child care, close confidant, household help, and financial partner. For those who have strained family relations, or who live far from relatives, survival is more difficult. The environment of Bogotá and all of Colombia has become so hostile that Bogotanos are hesitant to trust one another or to seek strangers' aid in times of need. Since residents have little institutional assistance available to them, those barrio residents in crisis without family or friends face desperation and even destitution.

Gender roles and family dynamics are also representative of mainstream Latin culture. Children are responsible for a heavy contribution of household chores and child care, and for their studies. Most girls are experienced cooks, maids, and nannies by their tenth or eleventh birthday. Grandparents are cared for within the home, and they also contribute as they are able. Women commonly bear the load of child raising and housework, often working full time as well outside the home. They have little free time, and many endure constant domestic violence and battering on top of their heavy loads. At the time of my stay, cooking and cleaning were done in traditional styles, for very few homes had ovens, washing machines, or hot water. Electricity and water were precarious and limited.

Though families vary, most men in Nuevo Progreso take responsibility for earning a salary, participating in barrio work parties, building a house for their family, and doling out physical punishment. Some work hard to contribute to the barrio's progress and to provide a future for their children. Others spend their salaries carousing about carelessly, arriving home drunk to make demands on the family and to cause fear and anger to resonate in the household. The machismo of Latin culture is still strong among the families of the working class, even though other traditional aspects have been lost in the new demands of city life.

Education is highly valued in Nuevo Progreso. Many in the older generations, having grown up in the countryside, were unable to attend school as children and often face employment obstacles for their lack of marketable skills. Determined to *seguir adelante* (continue ahead), some adults take Saturday classes or evening courses to finish their schooling or to gain new skills for employment. The emphasis on education is also reflected in many families who pay a substantial monthly *pensión* for their children's schooling, uniforms, and books. In spite of their hopes, however, the lack of opportunities is a strong discouragement to aspiring youth, and many drop out to become employed. They start families young, already with small children by the age of twenty, already trapped in low-wage, low-skill jobs.

In the evening, as the day winds down, parents and children often gather in a central room or a bedroom to have dinner, watch television, and do homework. Family members are hard on one another, for survival depends on the contribution of all. There is little sympathy for the weary or burdened member, for life is tough for everyone. However, they make incredible sacrifices for one another and share seemingly unbreakable ties. For in reality, only in the family do they find security, hope, and belonging.

Community Life

In demonstration of the earnest hope that is shared by Nuevo Progreso residents, progress and improvement are commonly visible throughout the barrio. On any given weekend or holiday, one can see many homes where the owners are busy working with their families:

> It's amazing to walk through the streets and alleyways, because there is a constant scene of progress. Several men pouring cement to make the foundation for the second floor. A family carrying bricks, stacking them to use when the adhesive mud is ready. A man in a hard hat and boots and ratty jeans mixing the

> yellow dirt with water in a steel container—slowly moving the
> shovel back and forth until there is a perfect texture. A man on
> his knees spreading cement in the front room of his house while
> his wife watches him, leaning in the doorway.
>
> —*Field Notes*

Home improvement is almost a unanimous goal among the barrio
residents. My host family added a second story to their home during
my stay, which included four bedrooms, a bathroom, and a kitchen.
Working bit by bit, as resources were available, my "dad" laid cement
walls and floors, installed windows and tile, and made a kitchen
counter and sink. Typical of other adult residents, he has only a first-
grade education and will probably always earn minimum wage.
However, his heart is proud and his hands are skilled, and his family's
future is his first priority.

Collective progress is also evident in the barrio as the residents
seek to improve their general living conditions and neighborhood
services. During my research, residents were planning the construction of a health clinic, and volunteers were being trained to adminis-
ter first aid there. Even with tens of thousands of residents, the barrio
did not yet have any emergency or preventative medical services.
Another committee was working on creating a barrio newspaper.
Work teams were constantly seen in the street, installing telephone
lines, redirecting water pipes, or preparing the street to be paved.

There were "block" meetings, committee elections, raffles, bingo
games, and a dozen volunteer nightwatch guards. A large elementary
school in the barrio offered free classes on topics ranging from math
to electricity and from flower arrangement to hair styling. Sometimes
there were mini soccer tournaments on a paved basketball court, with
teams, playoffs, and prizes. On Saturday mornings, a loudspeaker
blared with announcements and important news. Although the barrio's residents struggled with issues such as corruption, favoritism,
personal conflicts, and lack of resources in the neighborhood leadership, their ability to manage and plan for so many thousands of people with little government assistance was remarkable.

Due to Nuevo Progreso's distance from downtown Bogotá, it has
a fresh, countrylike atmosphere to it. The barrio is surrounded with
breathtaking scenery, and agricultural fields are but a short walk away.
The air is clean, pastureland is still abundant, and the houses are
newly built. There is not the dreariness of downtown Bogotá, where
one finds thick pollution, desperate prostitution, bands of street
orphans, violent homeless people, miles of cement, heavily armed law

enforcement, and the deafening roar of traffic. Residents of Nuevo Progreso find the distance to the city inconvenient, yet they appreciate the beauty and relative peacefulness of the barrio's location high in the mountains that surround Bogotá.

Lawlessness

Even with strong values of progress and individual responsibility in the barrio, delinquency and assault are not strangers to Nuevo Progreso. There are youth gangs that roam the barrio at night, attacking and robbing unsuspecting individuals, especially those who arrive home late from work or bars. Due to the absence of law enforcement in the barrio, and the lack of trust in government protection, residents often take matters into their own hands when they feel threatened. Murder, rape, assault, and theft occur almost unchecked, and victims have few resources with which to prosecute offenders.

Residents frequently told me of their encounters with danger in the barrio, and everyone knew of a neighbor or acquaintance who had been murdered right in the street close to their homes. One community mother I was visiting motioned toward a little girl in her day-care group whose mother had been shot in the face and killed while tending her shop. The father in the family I lived with had been held up at knifepoint several times while walking home from the bus. An evangelical family I knew listened to the murder of three young men outside their home one night who were attacked by an enemy gang. Another woman told me of her son who arrived home from school one day trembling, having seen a freshly killed youth with blood still spurting from his stab wounds. Residents casually mentioned seeing bodies on the street, attacked or shot. Nuevo Progreso has also experienced "social cleansing," in which youths suspected of crimes are taken from their homes in the middle of the night and shot by plainclothes law enforcement officers. No one protests, for fear of being the next victim. Despite its distance from the ruthless brutality of downtown Bogotá, Nuevo Progreso has not escaped the violence that permeates Colombia.

One can sense the desperation that barrio residents feel in the difficult circumstances of daily life because there are no easy solutions. For example, sometimes the barrio residents simply aren't paid by their employers, or have to work an entire weekend without pay under threat of termination. Due to the lack of affordable health care, children are born at home, herbal remedies used, and terrible pain endured. When family members leave for work or school, it's quite possible they won't come home alive. The tension and insecurity are so common that they become almost unnoticeable.

As a resident of the barrio, I was appalled at the casual regard for justice. With my own life at the mercy of the same destructive violence, I began to understand how powerless an individual can feel in such an environment. There is no protective structure, nor does one have resources to combat the danger or poverty. In employment, education, social mobility, and family welfare, the events of daily life are sculpted by giant brusque hands that oppress and burden. For those who live in barrios such as Nuevo Progreso, life is a giant rushing river, and survival requires sheer strength, determination, and hope.

Even after years of work and cooperation, Nuevo Progreso still needs large investments of labor and money to meet the residents' goals of public services, living conditions, safety, and general appearance. However, it is important to remember that there *are* goals and plans, which are being actively pursued. Despite the obstacles and circumstances of life in Nuevo Progreso, the people are not passive and fatalistic. They utilize community and family support and inner fortitude to *luchar* (struggle) and *salir adelante* (come out ahead), always in pursuit of a brighter future for themselves and their children.

Religious Life

The majority of Nuevo Progreso's population claim affiliation to the Roman Catholic Church, the dominant religion of Colombia. Until only a few years ago, an individual had to have official proof of baptism in the Catholic Church in order to obtain birth registration, admission into public schools, citizenship, employment, legal marriage status, and voting rights. Historically, Catholicism has held tremendous sway in the education, government, political and social affairs, justice, and cultural celebrations of Colombia. Until only recently, it was nearly impossible to separate the Colombian from his or her Catholic identity and worldview (see Haddox 1970:39).

Though Colombia remains the most traditional Catholic country in Latin America, the strength of the Church there is declining. This trend is reflected in Nuevo Progreso. Most residents of the barrio attend *misa* (mass) only a couple of times a year. They profess affiliation to the Catholic faith, yet do not participate in a church, to some extent because the opportunities for congregational worship and fellowship are limited.

In the entire barrio of one hundred thousand residents, there is only one Catholic church. It has one misa per week, at ten o'clock on Sunday mornings. The priest has under his charge six other churches in similar barrios, and is almost completely unavailable to the barrio residents for personal needs or spiritual guidance. Every Sunday morning, the little chapel fills with a couple hundred people, all standing because of the lack of pews. Without the aid of missals or music, they sing and recite prayers, meditate in silence, and listen to the homily. The service is over in fifty minutes.

Although church attendance is low among Catholics in the barrio, personal devotion is still evident. Many adorn their homes with prints of the Divino Niño Jesús (the Divine Child Jesus), believing that it has protective power over the household. Candles are kept lit, prayers are recited, and other *adornos* of Mary or the saints are kept in special household shrines. Infant baptism and first communion are commonly celebrated, and during Holy Week the church and its dirt courtyard are packed with Catholic believers. The catechism is taught in the barrio's schools, and it is common to hear children learning to recite prayers in a Saturday morning class.

In several places in Nuevo Progreso, statues of Mary and the baby Jesus have been erected. These are protected by small stone barriers and crudely decorated with flowers and lights. My host "mother" sometimes said good-bye to me with *"Que la Virgin la guarde"* (May the Virgin protect you), and she believed that Mary would help her through the labors of the day. When Marisol's[1] young daughter ran away, she prayed that the Virgin would help her find the girl, saying, "She knows what it's like to lose a child."

Since Mary and the saints are revered as having personable form, with human understanding and compassion, they receive the most prayers, special petitions, and devotion. Although all believe in God, the divine is perceived to be far away, inaccessible, and too busy to care for individual needs. Jesus is portrayed in church and home as either a child or a crucified man, discouraging the notion of a close relationship with him. Catholics in the barrio pray to the baby Jesus for certain needs, laying flowers at the foot of statues or pictures, but Jesus' divine power to intervene and change circumstances is perceived to be limited, infrequent, and even unexpected.

For supernatural intervention in a special situation, some residents openly seek the powers and advice of *brujería*, or witchcraft. In practices that can be traced to indigenous customs and the influence

---

[1]All names used in this study are pseudonyms chosen by the subjects.

of African slave culture in Colombia, spells are cast, visions seen and interpreted, potions mixed and slipped into drinks, and special rituals performed. Once I witnessed a "seer" tie male and female dolls together by candlelight, murmuring incantations. It was a ritual to bring about fidelity in the client's husband. This was carried out in the same household in which my "mother" would pray daily to the Virgin Mary. Such mixing of nominal Catholicism and casual spiritism is common in homes of Nuevo Progreso.

The Mystery of Spiritual Zeal

There is a small minority in the barrio that is not of Catholic affiliation. Some of these residents object to the traditional Catholic religion and have rejected all forms of religious practice. Others belong to the evangélico faith, which includes a style of worship known as Pentecostalism.

The Pentecostals make their presence known in the barrio, despite their minority status. Church meetings are frequent, and the doors of the church are always swung wide open as an invitation to curious passers-by who may be intrigued by the lively music or excited behavior inside. The believers engage in neighborhood evangelism, home meetings, and outside services, attempting to draw "sinners" from certain spiritual death and into life with God. Their fervent worship, eager evangelism, and claims to the supernatural have brought scorn and ridicule from barrio residents, but have also drawn a growing number of committed believers.

Although the evangélicos struggle through the same poverty and danger as all Nuevo Progreso residents do, their perception of life or worldview is almost completely guided by their intense religious faith. The transformation that takes place in conversion to the evangelical faith is so significant that the believers are readily noticeable by their distinct conduct, language, and passionate spirituality.

It is a remarkable sight to witness a Pentecostal meeting in one of the homes or small churches of the barrio. The *compañerismo* (fellowship) of the believers is comparable to the intimacy of a large family gathering. The spirited worship is at times like a pep rally and at other times wrought with soulful weeping and affection. Through observation of daily life and church attendance, it becomes clear that these believers embrace their faith not as a practice but as a *way of life*, an *identity*. Their religious fervor elicits questions that seek understanding: What is found within the faith that draws such an intense commitment from believers? How might barrio life, with its dangers and poverty, encourage the conversion of these believers? What can be so attractive about sobriety, fasting, and long church meetings?

Such is the strength of this movement that it has drawn considerable attention from academia. Many scholars have thus sought to answer this question: Why are Latin Americans converting to Pentecostalism?

A small church on the main street of the barrio—
the pastor's family lives on the second floor

3

The Mystery of the Movement

In February of 1996, I accompanied Carlos and Marisol on the hour-long bus ride from Nuevo Progreso to their church, Centro Misionero Internacional (CMI), in downtown Bogotá. When we arrived, the auditorium was packed full of thousands of believers, all with hands raised, singing, "Take me in to the Holy of Holies, by the blood of the redeeming Lamb." As the service progressed, we sang and danced with upbeat music, cheered for testified miracles, purged sickness and pain from our bodies through healing rituals, and heard a brief sermon about having spiritual anointing to heal others. Hung behind the podium was a great banner that read, "*10,000 Grupos Propósito Para 1996*," affirming the aggressive vision of the church: to have 10,000 home meetings established in Bogotá by the end of the year, each with an average of ten visitors.

At the end of the meeting, the pastor invited those who wished to repent and turn to Jesus to come forward. Over thirty-five individuals did so, and the congregation responded with thunderous applause. Marisol leaned over to me and whispered proudly, "This many people convert in every meeting." As we filed out, hundreds were already in line for the next *reunión*. CMI did meet its goal to have over 100,000 people under its spiritual leadership through church and home meetings in 1996. The church has since begun to use Bogotá's grand coliseum for its meetings, where tens of thousands can worship together at one time.

The extraordinary growth of CMI comes as no surprise to scholars, government leaders, and religious authorities, who have witnessed a similar wonder on a continent-wide scale for several decades now. More sectors of Latin American society are taking notice of the movement every year, for the influence of Pentecostalism has spread to politics, the media, economic development, commerce, education,

35

and even to the forgotten regions whose way of life is centuries old. From the Southern Cone to the U.S.-Mexico border, the presence of the evangélico faith is palpable and bold.

Curious minds from all fields of study and geographical regions have speculated on possible causes for the unprecedented appeal of the Pentecostal movement to the Latin American populace. Scholars have studied church history, social movements, evangelism strategies, politics and class issues, democracy, and modern forces of change. Understandably, there is a wide spectrum of ideas and theories. Close analysis reveals that most can be classified into three principal categories: structural, social, and spiritual.

Structural Change

During the decades of 1950 to 1970, Latin America experienced a period of massive urbanization and rapid modernization. No longer able to sustain their meager existence as *campesinos,* millions streamed in from rural areas to settle in the capitals and other urban sectors. Makeshift shantytowns grew on the peripheries of the cities, extending further and further to accommodate the overwhelming flood of migrants (Lindqvist 1972). Such changes disrupted traditional family structures and ways of life as the poor struggled to survive in their hostile, new, city environments (Westmeier 1986:22).

Studies of the evangélicos that were carried out during this period explain the growth of Pentecostalism in light of such massive structural changes. Emilio Willems examined Protestantism in Chile and Brazil in the early 1960s. His book *Followers of the New Faith* (1967) was a ground-breaking study of the growing movement. Willems hypothesized that the forces of modernization had weakened traditional values, creating an aperture for Protestantism. Agriculture was giving way to factories and urban jobs, women were entering the paid workforce, international trade was booming, and Latin culture was becoming exposed to foreign ideas and trends. Without such transformations, Pentecostal evangelization would have continued to struggle against centuries-old religious, societal, and cultural barriers.

Christian Lalive d'Epinay utilized structural theory in his book *Haven of the Masses* (1969) about Pentecostals in Chile. As a result of far-reaching societal changes, asserted Lalive, many members of the lower classes were being uprooted from the security of family and village ties in the migration to the cities. Without refuge or a means to cope with the threatening existence of sprawling urban areas, these people were seeking new community. Lalive described them as having "moral meaninglessness." "Pentecostalism appears as a communal religious answer to the confusion of large sections of the population, caused by the anomic character of a society in transition" (p. 15). The close-knit, supportive, family-like style of Pentecostal churches re-created for the migrants a community of social and material exchange not unlike the old hacienda from which they had come.

A similar study was conducted among the Quichua Indians in Ecuador. Conrad Kanagy (1990) discussed the economic and political difficulties of the Quichua community as structural forces began to transform their traditional social order. Faced with this crisis, they were open to the mission efforts of Protestants and through conversion were successfully organized to confront the changes. Everet A. Wilson, in his article "The Dynamics of Latin American Pentecostalism," also asserted that the new faith has had a special appeal for the populations most affected by changing economic patterns (1994:89).

The structural argument attributes Pentecostal growth to recent large-scale economic, political, and societal transformations in Latin America that have impacted hundreds of millions of people and their means of daily existence. Through the forces of industrialization and modernization, and the new challenges of urban life, many have lost their sense of identity and stability. As a result, they have sought belonging in a new "community." Scholars assert that Pentecostal churches have responded in kind to this need, drawing in the masses and thus growing at phenomenal rates.

Social Need

Historically, religion has drawn many devoted believers from the lower echelons of society. Its promises of hope, peace, and eternal life attract the powerless, the hopeless, the downtrodden, and the desperate poor, who seek meaning in their otherwise oppressive existence. Perhaps in the context of contemporary Latin America, the poor also seek physical and emotional survival in the evangélico churches.

The majority of Pentecostal believers in Central and South America are from the lower social classes, though the movement is reaching into the middle class (Berg and Pretiz 1994:14; Thornton 1981:98). One only needs to walk through a marginalized barrio or working-class neighborhood and see the fervent prayer of kneeling believers, high-spirited dancing and singing, and dynamic preaching in dozens of little churches to believe that Pentecostalism is truly the religion of the poor in Latin America (Stoll 1990:317; Willems 1967:205). Although Catholicism "opted for the poor" through

Liberation Theology, the masses have flocked to Pentecostal churches. "Pentecostal churches do not opt for the poor because they are
already a poor people's church. And that is why poor people are
choosing them" (Mariz 1994:80).

The social theory asserts that Pentecostal churches draw the marginalized poor by offering practical services that ease the strain of
daily life. The church acts as a social institution, giving attention to
the sick (through "divine healing") and providing food baskets, labor
pools, job networks, emergency funds (through "love offerings"), and
exchanges of goods such as clothing or furniture. Members of the
lower classes have frequent, pressing material needs, and the
Pentecostal churches offer solutions for these. In addition, the intimate unity within the church between hermanos provides social and
emotional support.

One excellent study of the practical purpose of religious community is Cecelia Mariz's *Coping with Poverty* (1994). From her research
among Pentecostal churches, Christian base communities, and Afro-
spiritist groups in northeastern Brazil, Mariz found that believers
were able to utilize practical survival strategies through membership
in the church community. "Pentecostalism creates an alternative network of support. For most Pentecostals, this informational network is
more helpful for their material survival than the institutional church
itself" (p. 93). Pentecostalism became a "strategy of coping with
poverty" because it legitimated practical behaviors that were function-
al for individual survival (p. 125).

Leslie Gill (1990) studied Pentecostal women in La Paz, Bolivia,
whom she described as "the poorest and most marginal residents of
the city" (p. 709). Joined together by a common set of beliefs in the
"Pentecostal experience," the women "construct new social networks
that are emotionally supportive and economically useful":

> These ties extend well beyond the church into the individuals'
> daily lives. Believers provide one another with information about
> living arrangements, jobs, medical assistance, and business oppor-
> tunities in the city, and they are readily available for assistance
> and support in times of crisis (p. 713).

Steigenga (1994) found that a large sector of Guatemala's poor
have found new survival strategies through Protestantism, as traditional strategies have become obsolete (p. 144; also Stoll 1990:331). A
Colombian evangelical summarized it well in Thornton's study: "They
gave me a sense of belonging, and they were ready to help in my time
of need" (1981:63).

The lack of government assistance in the struggle of the marginalized poor in Latin America leaves a void both in the community and in individuals' sense of protection and security. The social argument asserts that Pentecostal churches fill this void by acting like a social institution for many, reinforcing family values and caring for the well-being of their congregations. Not only do the believers become part of a valuable resource network, but they also receive encouragement and support as members of the church family.

Spiritual Fulfillment

The third major explanation for Pentecostal growth in Latin America has to do with the eternal search for spiritual fulfillment. As Berger states in *The Sacred Canopy* (1967), "The religious enterprise of human history profoundly reveals the pressing urgency and intensity of man's quest for meaning" (p. 100). Kelley affirms that "man is an incorrigibly religious creature who wants to make sense out of his life" (1972:37). Harvey Cox, professor of religion at Harvard University, spent time in Latin America as he researched his book about Pentecostalism, *Fire from Heaven* (1995). During a discussion over lunch with nuns, priests, sociologists, theologians, and pastors, Cox realized that the believers' desire for something is a crucial part in understanding the power of the movement:

> However vaguely or incoherently, they yearned for something—healing, fellowship, salvation, empowerment, dignity, meaning, serenity, ecstasy—they saw in other people, and decided to claim it for themselves; then, having done so, they became the glad bearers of its message (p. 182).

Scholars have speculated that several "spiritual" factors have contributed to the dissemination of Pentecostalism. First, Latin culture has increasingly been exposed to foreign religions and faiths, creating a religious marketplace where seekers can experiment, visit different churches, and even combine beliefs (Berryman 1995). In this pluralistic environment, Pentecostal churches can evangelize freely and emphasize the attractions of their faith to others, thus adding to the membership rolls.

Second, Latin American culture is, by nature, passionate and spiritual (see Mackay 1932, Stoll 1990). The widespread practice of African spiritism, divination, saint worship, superstition, and folk religion demonstrates a common belief in the supernatural. Karl

Wilhelm Westmeier described it as the "popular mystical piety" (1986:19) in his work among Colombians. In this light, it is no wonder that Pentecostalism has drawn people with its extraordinary miracles, encounters with the demonic realm, and spiritual manifestations such as speaking in tongues or being "slain in the Spirit."

Third, due to the insufficient number of Catholic clergy in booming Latin America, the leadership and influence of the Catholic Church over the continent has weakened considerably. This void of pastoral care and religious community has sent millions of disillusioned Latin Americans in search of other forms of spiritual fulfillment, especially to evangelical churches. In 1985, there were 15,000 full-time Protestant pastors in Brazil compared to 13,176 priests (Martin 1990:50–51). This means that there was one priest for every 14,000 Catholics and one pastor for every 1,600 evangelicals. Between 1990 and 1992, the Instituto de Estudos da Religiao documented the opening of 710 new Protestant churches (90 percent of them Pentecostal) in the Rio de Janeiro area. During the same two years, one new Catholic parish was opened (Fernandes 1992; cf. Berryman 1995:109).

As the Catholic Church has struggled internally through social, political, and hierarchical issues, Pentecostal churches have been earnestly evangelizing on street corners and in healing revivals, growing by the millions. Over thirty years ago, Houtart and Pin wrote about the revolutionary changes occurring in Latin America (1965). Their evaluation of pastoral deficiencies in the Catholic leadership was prophetic.

In an unstable time of economic hardship, political corruption, and social unrest, millions of Latin Americans have turned to Pentecostal churches for personal spiritual guidance and fulfillment. Using the spiritual theory, scholars attribute the continued growth of Pentecostalism to the weakening Catholic influence and the emerging pluralistic religiosity in Latin America. They also point to the Pentecostal churches' exuberant worship, Biblical instruction, family environment, individual spiritual guidance, and emphasis on supernatural encounters (Westmeier 1986, Deiros and Mraida 1994, Wilson 1994).

But What About the Religion?

As shown above, the majority of existing studies that explain the appeal of Pentecostalism to lower-class Latin Americans can be classified into the three general theories of structural, social, and spiritual.

All are valid explanations that have been supported through field-work and data analysis. These theories create a solid foundation from which to examine how the religious landscape of Latin America has evolved in recent decades and the changing spiritual needs of the greater population. They also accurately explain the initial attraction of individuals to the evangelical faith.

With respect to the evangelical faith, however, the existing literature lacks several important elements that are crucial to understanding the movement's strength among Latin Americans. First, it seems that social scientists have explored every issue pertinent to the causes and effects of Pentecostalism in Latin America, without actually studying the faith itself. A broad spectrum of topics has been covered, from macrostructural causes (Kanagy 1990) to the movement's history (de Bucana 1995), from democratic implications (Smith 1994) to transformed gender roles (Brusco 1995), and from political conspiracy (Stoll 1990) to evangélicos' community participation (Flora 1976). While these concepts are all important to understanding the origins and influence of Pentecostalism in the greater society, a void of knowledge still remains that begs for information about the *elements and exercise of the religion in question.*

Speaking metaphorically, it would seem that researchers have examined the car's exterior and peered through the windows, remarking at the strength of its tires, the loaded options, and versatility of its use, and drawing conclusions about the landscape, road, and weather conditions without looking under the hood or getting inside. The appeal of the object is certain, but questions remain: What is its source of power? What is the view from the inside? And what are the elements of its use that draw such devotion from so many millions of people? Although contextual research is valuable and informative, it does not provide a complete picture.

Simply stated, to study a religion, we must study the religion itself. If we understand the motives and passions of believers' hearts and congregations, we then can draw valuable conclusions about the religion's influence in greater society. Furthermore, the faith must be examined from within, through the believers' perspective, instead of from without, which is the secular perspective, to truly depict the strength of the faith in believers' lives. For the average Latin American Pentecostal, dressed in humble attire, hands clasped in emotion, eyes closed, singing "*Jesús es todo para mí*" to the slow strum of an electric guitar, conversion means new life, peace, protection, and security. God and his love are real for the believers, and it is important to recognize this in the field of research.

The second area that needs further study is the issue of believers' *commitment* to the Pentecostal faith. A review of the existing literature shows that structural, social, and spiritual theories only give valid explanations for the initial, temporary attraction of the Pentecostal faith. Driven by a felt need such as a sick child, unemployment, insecurity, or loneliness, individuals are attracted by the promise of immediate spiritual or material resolution in the church. While this appeal may indeed play a part in drawing visitors and even converts to the faith, it does not explain why individuals maintain high levels of devotion and sacrifice to the faith years after the initial need has been forgotten. The image of the Pentecostal church as a cash machine of sorts where people can make free withdrawals and get their emotional and material needs met is mistaken. A quick review of the demanding weekly church activities and strict moral codes would discourage all those who are only looking for free handouts or network benefits. Commitment to the religion is a serious decision that has the power to transform an individual's identity, worldview, and life purposes. What is the central motivation for remaining a devoted believer to a religion whose followers have historically endured persecution, social ostracism, and personal sacrifice?

Third, very few studies exist that dually explore the intimate elements of the faith and their practical and spiritual role in the daily lives of the believers. As demonstrated in research, the evangélico faith enjoys the greatest success in the population of the large working class, whose existence is focused upon getting by in an unstable and oppressive environment. I would argue that this correlation between socioeconomic level and religious preference arises from the strong relationship between daily struggle and evangélico church practices. Any observer will note that the believers' heavy emotional burdens are lifted and lost during worship services, and that biblical principles learned in church are relevant and applicable to the situations faced when the believers return home. They live to follow Jesus and they follow Jesus to live. This complex interplay between home life and church participation must be explored. Examined as separate elements, the importance of one's influence on the other, which is essentially the mainspring of the faith, is overlooked.

In response to the need for deeper insight into this faith, the study at hand seeks to present an intimate view of Pentecostal believers in Bogotá, examining the elements of conversion, commitment, and faith maintenance through church and daily life activities. Furthermore, it will illuminate the components of the believers' strong devotion to God and the church with two concepts that are specific to the experience of individuals in the faith.

Worldview

Lofland and Stark (1973) wrote, "All men and all human groups have ultimate values, a world view, or a perspective furnishing them a more or less orderly and comprehensive picture of the world" (p. 28). Luckmann called this worldview a "moral universe of meaning" (1967:51), and Kearney "a way of looking at reality" (1984:41). In his study of Colombian Protestants, Thornton called it "how one views himself, his relation to others and his relation to society and the world in general" (1981:46).

One's worldview is formed by the surrounding subculture through the process of socialization. As a child grows in an environment within a certain language, way of life, and social stratum, and with specific customs and beliefs, he or she learns to understand and interpret daily life and the world through the lens of the group's worldview. The child's worldview is collectively produced and reinforced by the influences in the surrounding environment. For example, a street orphan from Rio de Janeiro views the world differently than a British aristocrat. For one, reality is the endless fight to survive among wretched poverty, filth, and physical danger. The other, surrounded with luxury and importance, can be concerned with social and political affairs that mean nothing or everything to millions of people.

Although a worldview takes years to be sculpted and shaped by one's environment, it is constantly subject to influence and change. On one hand, an individual's worldview may be simply strengthened and reinforced by consistent influence in a singular environment. On the other hand, it may be transformed by a new experience, a profound life event, a different environment, or changed circumstances. I would argue that one's worldview is ultimately dynamic, daily influenced, and constantly molded by all that surrounds and touches his or her existence. In order to continually hold to a specific set of beliefs and principles, that worldview needs constant maintenance and reinforcement.

In the preceding chapter, we explored the life of the barrio in this study: the families, jobs, community, history, and daily struggle. The worldview of the residents in Nuevo Progreso is shaped by the difficult circumstances that they endure from childhood to old age. Insecurity, disappointment, determination, and inner fortitude are instilled and reinforced in individuals by the hardships of violence and poverty in everyday life. Feeling no protection from government or community, and tenuous care from divine images in Catholicism, the residents battle forces that threaten their family's well-being as a solitary flower against a heavy rainstorm or a beaver's dam against a rushing river. They cling to sources of hope and strength as a lifeline, but despite these efforts, the endless burdens are manifested in tears and weariness.

The residents love laughter, celebration, and times of enjoyment, and are a generous, affectionate people. Their general worldview is a product of the subculture of Nuevo Progreso as a working-class barrio in a Latin American metropolis. This worldview is also collectively reinforced by the music, family, community, and daily life of the barrio. It is a lens through which all things are seen and understood.

Through religious conversion, an individual's worldview necessarily changes. The transformation experienced by converts is not otherworldly, as though they become unattached to family, community, daily life, and reality, living in a strange spiritual euphoria. Rather, it is otherworldly in that converts begin to view every aspect of their lives through the lens of the spiritual realm. The struggles continue, but believers interpret their purpose and resolution through the all-encompassing evangélico worldview. The revelation that is experienced is best illustrated by the following Bible story, found in chapter 6 of 2 Kings.

Elisha, a prophet of God, had been thwarting the battle plans of the king of Aram through his divine revelations of the king's every strategic move. Enraged, the king set out to capture Elisha at Dotham, where the prophet and his servant were staying. Verses 15–17 read: "When the servant of the man of God got up and went out early the next morning, an army with horses and chariots had surrounded the city. 'Oh, my lord, what shall we do?' the servant asked. 'Don't be afraid,' the prophet answered, 'Those who are with us are more than those who are with them.' And Elisha prayed, 'O Lord, open his eyes so he may see.' Then the Lord opened the servant's eyes, and he looked and saw the hills full of horses and chariots of fire all around Elisha."

In a moment of terrible crisis, the servant became distraught. His perception of the situation was that an entire army was encamped against two men. He expected certain death or brutal captivity. Elisha the prophet was not afraid of the apparent odds, for in his vision, the heavenly army of fiery chariots and horses was far more powerful and numerous. The servant's revelation of this supernatural force radically changed his interpretation of the situation, and his resulting behavior. He was not removed from the crisis; no, the army was still encamped to take their lives. Yet he had caught glimpse of the unseen heavenly fortress that would act on their behalf, and in this assurance of strength and security, his whole outlook or worldview would never be the same.

Latin American Pentecostalism is like Elisha, and the masses of poor and working-class people are like the servant. Through conversion and subsequent steps of commitment to the faith, individuals are taught that a powerful, benevolent God, his son Jesus, his Spirit, and all his angels seek to act on behalf of God's children, or Christians. Wickedness, poverty, and violence are believed to originate from the demonic realm of Satan, with whom one must contest in the battle over physical health, jobs, family well-being, and salvation of the world. Although Latin Americans are made aware of the spiritual realm by their culture, in Pentecostalism this awareness becomes a way of life.

The transformation experienced through conversion is radical, affecting every aspect of the convert's identity, behavior, and life purposes. This is so because change has occurred in the most fundamental element of one's being: the worldview. Personality and lifestyle can be altered rather temporally and even superficially, but once the mind has been imbued with profound convictions of eternity and life, the change that follows is serious and often permanent.

As mentioned previously, the barrio residents' worldviews are collectively produced and maintained by the influences of the surrounding subculture. Their interpretation of life events and daily situations is guided by what they learn through family, community, and media. When an individual converts to the Pentecostal faith and undergoes a radical change in worldview, this new interpretation of life events and daily situations must be also collectively and continuously reinforced by the evangélico community. Worldview adherence is essentially socially dependent.

The believers' continued commitment is determined by the strength of their religious worldview, for when the tangible or intangible incentives for membership are perceived to be shallow or unworthy of continued commitment, personal zeal ebbs and the convert falls away from the faith. The shared worldview that one gains through conversion is extremely dynamic, subject to intensification and strengthening, or discouragement and dilution. Without constant buttressing of the believers' faith and convictions, contrary influences outside the church can gain a foothold in drawing them away.

Rational Choice

"Rational," as defined by the *American Heritage Dictionary*, is "consistent with or based on reason; logical." When surrounded by the swords and fighting men of the Aramian army, Elisha's servant had a logical reaction: pure fright. That would be the natural response of any individual who calculates the odds according to that which is seen or perceived by the senses. For example, when a barrio resident measures the increased cost of living against a cut in wages, the reasonable conclusion is that her family must reduce their living standard or find additional employment.

However, Elisha's next course of action would not be rational to an individual who had no perception of the supernatural power behind the prophet. Elisha prayed that God would blind the eyes of the entire Aramian army. Only a fool would hope for such an unlikely miracle in the face of great odds. In the story, God blinded their eyes, and Elisha led them into a city hostile to the Aramians. He fed the soldiers and released them in peace, and the king of Aram ceased his persecution of the Israelite nation.

The implication here is that Pentecostals, acting on their perception of the supernatural, will make choices and act in ways that seem irrational to the nonevangelical but are perfectly natural for those who share the belief. Their strategies for daily survival take on a new rationale, as do the resolutions that they seek for difficult situations. Facing pressing bills, believers will tithe money to the church. Facing unemployment, they may fast and pray for a week. To the outsider, these choices are nonsensical and even fatalistic. To the believer, they are empowering, inspiring, and a demonstration of love to God.

The rational choice theory asserts that believers choose their religious affiliation and any subsequent actions in daily life based on what they perceive to be rational and logical, all of which is guided by their worldview. During the conversion process, believers become exposed to and acquire the supernatural worldview of the evangélico faith. This transforms their perception of what is rational behavior. The new worldview is then manifested in the choices carried out in life struggles and events. As we delve deeper into the study, the reader will find that this theory explains initial conversion, strong commitment, daily devotion, and even falling away from the faith.

The rational choice theory is distinct from prevailing themes in religious studies today. Instead of attributing personal faith to great societal influences, it focuses on the personal decisions of individuals as the agent of religious affiliation. A look at the existing literature reveals a tendency of scholars to explain individual religious faith by pointing to structural forces of an entire continent (decline of the Catholic Church, urbanization, modernization, and economic crises). Although these forces play a crucial part in influencing the religious options available and their appeal to the masses, in the end, it is the individual who chooses to believe or not, to commit to the religion or to reject it. The surrounding subculture may influence the individual to perceive a religion in one way or another, but it cannot enforce personal belief.

Worldview and rational choice theories give the baton back to the individual believer whose own heart holds the passion of faith, devotion, and the zeal to reach the world with Jesus' love.

In light of this discussion, the question asked at the end of Chapter 2—Why are Latin Americans converting to Pentecostalism?—is more appropriately phrased, What do Latin Americans perceive in the Pentecostal faith that causes conversion, commitment, and radical worldview transformation? How are believers motivated to make incredible sacrifices of time and resources to the faith? Furthermore, how is the Pentecostal worldview taught and reinforced to maintain the believers' strength and devotion in the faith? Herein lie many of the intimate elements of this religious movement's strength and influence over the lives of millions of believers.

The first steps of worldview transformation are accomplished on the path to conversion, which is the crucial foundation of membership in the Pentecostal movement. This genesis of individual faith will be explored in the next chapter.

The alabanza, *or spirited worship music*

4
"Arriving at the Feet of Jesus": The Path to Conversion

Tantas cosas han pasado	Many things have happened
Desde que yo conocí a mi Señor	Since I met my Lord
Me ha cambiado la manera	He has changed my way
De hablar y de cantar,	Of talking and singing,
De vestir y caminar	Of dressing and walking
En esta vida.	In this life.
Y si hablo de milagros	And if I speak of miracles
Y de tantas cosas bellas	And of so many beautiful things
Que Tú me has dado	That You have given me
No termino este día	I won't finish this day
De contar las tantas cosas	Counting the many things
Que me has regalado Tú.	That You have given to me.

Sung by Angela in her interview, March 15, 1996

S ince the early 1970s, the rise of millenarian and UFO cults, spiritual communes, Eastern religions, and various authoritarian sects has drawn the interest and inquiry of the public and the media. Scholars of sociology, psychology, and religious studies have responded with an impressive quantity of studies on the topic of religious conversion and commitment (Snow and Machalek 1984:167–168). Attention given to the phenomena increased so dramatically that the decade of the 1970s has been called "the age of conversion" (Richardson and Stewart 1977:24).

Because the focus of study has ranged from the Unification Church, known as the "Moonies" (DeMaría 1978), to the Charismatic Renewal among Catholics (Harrison 1975), to Hare Krishna, a Hindu consciousness group (Ullman 1989), it is not surprising that there is a wide variety of definitions for the term "religious conversion." They vary along a spectrum to the degree of change required to join a religion. For some, conversion may only be a necessary prerequisite for an interfaith marriage, which entails little adjustment in the individual's worldview or environment. For others, it may involve the complete abandonment of job, family, home, possessions, and identity (see Balch and Taylor 1977 in their study of a UFO cult), as converts are drawn into hiding, wandering, or even mass suicide.

In this study of Pentecostals in Bogotá, religious conversion can be described as a balance between the two extremes. Converts maintain their responsibilities to family, job, and home, continuing the struggle of daily life amidst an environment of poverty and danger. Yet they experience radical personal transformation, which guides them into viewing the world and daily events with a totally new perspective. The converts' behavior, appearance, and rationale follow in accordance with this new worldview, visibly setting them apart from their nonevangelical neighbors and family members.

Evangelical believers in Nuevo Progreso likened their conversion to awakening after a great slumber, or receiving sight for the first time. Some portrayed it as a bridge, where one crosses from ignorance and death into knowledge and life. For others, conversion was a balm of healing for a broken life, a light of guidance, or a crucial piece that had been missing. Since all their stories point to personal change as the shared theme, I prefer to describe conversion as similar to the transformation of a caterpillar into a butterfly.

The process of change from a caterpillar to a butterfly seems simple to the observer. First a colorful, fuzzy little creature is seen crawling about, and after a mysterious retreat into the cocoon, a gorgeous winged insect emerges. In its most elementary form, religious conversion has three stages identical to the butterfly process. Yet if we were to examine the complex biological transformation that occurs within the cocoon, we would be filled with wonder and appreciation for the radical nature of the change. So it is in the study of religious conversion.

In the following pages, we will explore the gradual stages of conversion to the evangelical faith. We begin with the caterpillar, which is the lifestyle, worldview, and interests of individuals before joining the faith. Next the cocoon will be examined, which represents the five principal elements in the path to conversion. The climactic moment of conversion follows. Finally, we will discuss the new life purposes and worldview of the butterfly, or convert, and the changing motives for devotion to the faith.

The Caterpillar: A Starting Point

Why study the caterpillar, or the pre-convert? The butterfly is a beautiful creature, but its existence becomes wondrous and awesome once the student learns of its undistinguished origin. Likewise, the believer with a worn Bible and devoted lifestyle may be inspiring. However, when we take into account her rough or miserable background, the life-changing significance of conversion becomes tangible and impressive.

As discussed in Chapter 2, there are several key components that influence the worldview of the barrio residents: family, daily survival, surrounding culture, and the Catholic faith. The common thread woven through over one hundred thousand lives in Nuevo Progreso is an oppressive and burdensome existence. Child and adult alike carry physical and emotional burdens from insecurity, violence, poverty, and powerlessness. Networks of support are fragile and inconsistent. Hardship knocks relentlessly at the brightly painted doors of the barrio homes, carrying bundles of scarcity, loneliness, and pain.

Refuge and hope are found in family and distant dreams. Quick wit and humor is common, for the residents enjoy laughter and good fellowship. Though their lives are clearly defined by the requirements for survival, few resist a moment to be with close friends or family over some *tinto* and *pan* (black coffee and bread). Sources of strength and peace such as these are clung to as life buoys. Social progress is a common goal, yet all are aware of the precarious nature of life and the future. The residents live each day to provide a warm meal to the family in the evening, to keep a roof over their heads, and to come out ahead in spite of all opposition. Through all of this, the Catholic religion is protected as sacred, excluding other beliefs, yet having little impact on the residents' daily existence.

The following is the story of two believers in this study, exemplifying the stormy nature of many lives before finding the evangelical faith.

Marisol, a petite factory worker with long curls and a doll face, was prohibited from attending school as a child. Her family saw no use in her education. Viewed as a burden, she was sent away to be a full-time maid at age ten. Marisol's employer abused her so severely that she ran away to Venezuela. There, at age fourteen, she became mistress to a violent married man and bore his child a year later. She moved back to Bogotá, and with no education was forced to work as a live-in maid to support her little girl. Years down the road, after many degrading jobs and endless sacrifice, she met Carlos.

Carlos had recently emerged from street life, where he spent twelve years as a gang member immersed in drugs, filth, and crime. Marisol's sisters told her that as a single mother she'd never do better than Carlos. Since she had always longed for a complete, caring family, Marisol moved in with Carlos. Knowing only violence and deceit, he beat her brutally, such that she was unable to leave the home and be seen by others. Carlos degraded Marisol, constantly abusing her sexually and mentally. She in turn hated him, but had no place to turn. Eventually they had a son together, and struggled for years to maintain the home, battling in constant hostility and violence. Marisol and Carlos were in the midst of this situation when the evangelical faith took root in their lives.

Marisol and Carlos's story may sound miserable, but it is not unusual. It is important to emphasize that the worldview of barrio residents approaching the evangelical faith is largely shaped by the undesirable living conditions of the working poor. The caterpillar stage is marked by hardship. It is also characterized by general aversion to the evangelical movement.

Many social and cultural barriers lie in the path to the evangelical faith. These draw their strength from centuries of enforced religious affiliation among the Latin people. In spite of growing pluralism in Latin American religion, those who convert to Pentecostalism are often ridiculed, ostracized, and called traitors to the "mother faith" of Catholicism. It is no casual matter to visit a Pentecostal church as though one were "church shopping," as is common in the United States. The very mention of interest in the evangélico faith is sufficient cause for a heated discussion or severed relationships. Families are often divided over opposing religious allegiances. The reluctance expressed in joining an evangelical community is also understandable when one considers the high level of commitment that membership requires. In addition, there are widely held myths about Pentecostalism, originating from hostile interfaith relations, that keep Catholics a fair distance from their evangélico neighbors.

Individuals may approach the evangelical faith with skepticism, curiosity, or sheer emotional exhaustion. Their impression thus far has been shaped by a world that is unsympathetic to the faith and even less compassionate toward the working poor. As we now delve into the stages of transformation, or the cocoon, we can recall the toughened, longing heart of the pre-convert.

Elements of Conversion: The Cocoon

Scholars of religious conversion will agree that the range and variety of religious conversion is so extensive that a different book could be written for each individual experience. Likewise, in this study, each believer's story is as distinct as a handwoven Colombian tapestry with lively colors and images. In spite of their diversity, all conversions share a few principal components, as all tapestries do: structure, progression, and the final binding knot.

There are five principal elements, encountered in any sequence, that lead to the final step of conversion: predisposing life circumstances, contact with an evangelical, contact with a church, hearing the message of salvation, and experiencing the supernatural. All play an influential role in the decision to convert, although in some cases a single incident may be the deciding factor. In most cases, the five elements compound one another, intensifying the individual's desire to "arrive at Jesus' feet" and become an evangélico.

Peter Berger calls conversion "an individual transference into another world" (1967:50) and Turner and Killian define it as "a transfer of loyalty and total acceptance of beliefs" (1957:335). In the context of this study, I will analyze conversion as a progression of events that radically transform an individual's identity and worldview and lead him or her to embrace religious commitment. Here I will define each of these five elements, using believers' own words to illustrate the path to religious change.

Predisposing Life Circumstances

Predisposing life circumstances are those events or situations, experienced long- or short-term, which incline an individual to be more receptive to the proselytizing efforts of evangelical churches and believers. Macrostructural theories of conversion point to modernization, urbanization, economic strain, and weakening Catholic influence as a few of the widespread predisposing circumstances that have led to Pentecostal growth. Examined on the microlevel, they may also include the death of a loved one, loss of a job, constant domestic violence, a grave physical ailment, or the sudden absence of physical and emotional security, giving an individual a sense of need for the refuge and hope of the faith.

Sometimes, a single traumatic, eye-opening event triggers the desire for personal change and conversion. Such was the case with Abraham. Married, with two daughters, Abraham spent much time and precious wages away from home drinking and carousing with women. He would not recount to me the details from this period, saying, "It gives me shame to remember all I did." The home was constantly filled with tension, violent arguments, and economic strain. Late one night, on his way home from a bar, he was attacked by a youth gang and brutally beaten. Left for dead, he slowly crawled home, his head and shirt covered with blood. The beating served as a wake-up call for Abraham. He became convinced that his life in its present course had been destined to end in such a violent way, but that God had spared him so he could find salvation.

Ximena was also drawn during a short, desperate time in her life: "I converted because I became pregnant without being married. My sister began to talk to me about the Lord, and that's how I came to the Lord, because of my pregnancy. The father of the baby was far away, so I looked for a refuge and it was in God." In her midteens, the youngest in an impoverished family of twelve children, Ximena had nowhere to turn when she became pregnant. Not only did she find strength through her new faith, but she also joined a church with a strong, supportive women's group and an efficient resource network.

Latiana converted during her late teens. She had begun to run with the "bad" crowd of kids who were involved with drugs and delinquency in the street. Then a horrifying discovery was made. One of her friends was found cut to pieces in the most dangerous part of downtown Bogotá and was hardly recognizable. "At that moment, the Lord called me," Latiana recalled.

Luisa, a gray-haired woman with six grown children, converted as an adolescent when she and her father ventured into an evangelical church in search of healing for his malignant tumor. He was not healed, but there Luisa found a faith that she would follow passionately for the next forty years. Elías was in a religious festival one night in his hometown on the coast of Colombia when a girl standing right beside him was killed by an errant fireworks explosion. That very night he went to an evangélico service and committed his life to the faith.

Whereas some converts become open to the gospel message of the evangelicals in a brief, climactic period of time, others endure months or years of hardship before seeking desperate resolution in the faith. An example of this is Angela's story. She and her husband, an attractive and outgoing couple, were the life of the party in their youth. She sang, drank, danced, and flirted with men, spurred on by their attention and by her own desire to be the prettiest, the happiest, and the most wanted. Angela and her husband lived extravagantly, in spite of their working-class status:

> But behind all this, there was nothing. There was only a fantasy.
> In my heart there was no peace, because while I danced and flirted, there was always a fear of my husband. It seemed that I was living with a tiger. Because my husband was very jealous, too jealous,

very *machista,* a fighter, a drunk, a smoker. He got drunk a great deal, so when he came home to me we had many problems. We fought, we argued over everything, we treated each other with violence, with a lot of aggression, with bad words. There was no respect. He would say one bad word, I would say ten. He'd hit me and I'd hit him. Even in my pregnancies, he beat me a lot. In this life I lived, there was an emptiness. So when I came to the Lord, I felt that God changed my life.

When Angela received "the call," she converted right away, and her husband followed within the same week. Many believers, in recounting their stories, spoke of the pre-conversion time as fraught with anxiety, sadness, loneliness, anger, or difficulty (see Willems 1967:129). These times of crisis served as an impetus to seek change and hope within the evangelical faith.

When Olga was separating from her husband, facing the burden of single parenthood, an evangelical friend spoke to her about God. Olga felt immediately drawn to the faith. "She told me, 'He'll give you strength and ability,' and right away I said yes." Pedro was initially attracted to Pentecostalism by its claims of divine healing because his father had been stabbed and Pedro was desperate to save his father's life. When the basis of one's existence is threatened, the price of hope never seems too high. Even acceptance of a religion that demands self-surrender and commitment becomes a desirable option if it promises comfort and strength to the one in need.

Predisposing circumstances are nothing more than the normal struggles of everyday life in the barrio, unless there is a link to the evangelical faith that provides the individual with the opportunity to seek help there. Potential converts often come to perceive the faith as a desirable option through the evangelistic efforts of a believer they know personally.

Contact with an Evangélico

One generally comes into contact with an active evangélico within the intimate boundaries of his or her own home, extended family, or friendship network. Most evangelism takes place through established relationships between believers and nonevangelicals (see Glock 1973:42; Gerlach and Hine 1970:79,110; Snow and Machalek 1984:182). A Pentecostal is more likely to evangelize her husband, sister, neighbor, co-worker, or daughter-in-law before she will speak through a megaphone in the street or proselytize door-to-door. Daily life offers many opportunities of contact with those in one's own social network, and words about faith in Jesus or church activities slip into normal conversation quite naturally. Through these private, non-threatening channels, those who are interested in the faith can inquire, learn, and understand what it is to be an evangélico.

Catholic traditions are strong in Colombia, and evangélicos are still viewed as "crazies" by many Catholics. In an environment as insecure as Bogotá, very little trust exists between strangers. Individuals are skeptical of and even hostile toward those evangélicos who come proselytizing at their doorstep. A family member or close friend, however, has a distinct advantage in that sharing and openness already exist, and the "message of salvation" is close and personal.

To share their faith, believers seek to maintain exemplary lives of strict moral conduct in home and work, showing love, forgiveness, and self-restraint, so that family members, friends, and neighbors will be convinced and converted by the sincerity of their faith. They call it *"dando buen testimonio"* (giving good testimony). When nonevangelical friends or relatives encounter difficult or hopeless situations, the Pentecostals often utilize the situation as an opportunity to share their faith in God. It is in these times of despair, they believe, that people will be most aware of their need for God's love.

Among the forty-nine conversion stories that I collected in the interviews, 90 percent of the believers were initially evangelized by a family member, spouse, neighbor, or friend. For example, when Enrique would visit his mother-in-law, she would sit him down in the kitchen and speak to him about the *Palabra* (Bible). Latiana's aunts would go to her house with their Bibles, eager to answer her questions about God, Mary, and Jesus. Eduardo and Liliana rented a small room from evangelicals as newlyweds, and were surprised to wake up to sounds of fervent prayer in the early hours of the morning. Monica, a young mother from the Colombian countryside, lived in constant fear of her violent husband until they also were evangelized as tenants in a believer's home:

> So we were going to separate, because my husband hit me a lot and perhaps could kill me. But the Lord had a beautiful plan. We moved into a believer's house who spoke to us. He said, "I'll rent to you, but here I don't like the secular music. Here I don't like the *groserías* (bad language), none of that. Here it is holy. I don't want to hear any of that." We were there two weeks when he invited us to church. And he explained the Word to us, it was wonderful.

Andrés, a cook for the elite club of the Colombian army in Bogotá, converted through the "testimony" of his wife Diana. He had left her shortly after the birth of his daughter to go work far away, for several years. His wife recounted to me how she fasted and prayed for his salvation and return. Her patience was rewarded, as Andrés told me:

> I converted through my señora. When I met her, she already knew the Lord, but she returned to the ways of God when her sister passed away. When I came back, I knew that she was attending the church. I didn't like it, but had always respected the religion. So she invited me, and I began to go. I went one weekend and I liked it.

Several of my interviewees decided to convert after witnessing the radical change of someone they knew who became a believer. Having previously known the person as drunk, violent, vulgar, or die-hard Catholic, they were astonished by the change and became more receptive to the message of the evangelical faith. Roxana was living with her mother in the *campo* when she heard that a friend had converted:

> One time this guy went to Bogotá and came back married to a lady pastor, and he became a pastor. I couldn't believe it, so I got myself ready and went to the church to make fun of him. It impacted me so much that he was up there with a Bible. I looked for a chance to laugh at him. The service passed, and they prayed and sang. The lady pastor came over and put her arm around me and said, "I love you in the love of Christ." And I was surprised. I began to like it. I said, "There is something here."

Roxana was drawn by the change her friend had experienced, and she desired the love that was shared with her during the service. She was so convinced of its reality, through her friend's testimony, that she converted, went on to Bible school, married, established several churches around Bogotá, and finally became an evangelical pastor.

Contact with an evangelical is often the appealing "bait" for an individual to visit a Pentecostal church. The environment of the church plays a decisive role in the individual's progression toward conversion, since its worship services are literally designed to draw in new converts. The powerful dynamics of song, ritual, and gathered community leave a lasting impression in the minds of believers and nonbelievers alike.

Contact with a Church

Initial contact with a Pentecostal church can be a disturbing one for a nominal Catholic accustomed to the brief routine of the weekly mass. Warmth and welcome are lavished onto the newcomer, as well as a subtle degree of pressure to join the faith. The rousing cries of glory and victory, fists in the air, resemble something of a pep rally. Soulful emotions are expressed through the long hour of elated worship, as hermanos dance and spin in song, or weep and cry out with moving tones of sadness or humility. In larger churches, the music of a full band is often accompanied by dancers who move gracefully in choreographed perfection, swirling colored scarves above their heads. All believers pray out loud with the pastor, using their own words, creating a rather confusing flood of noise and voices. Sermons, called *mensajes* (messages), are long and animated, often energized with miracle works, and punctuated by the believers' cries of "Amen" or "*Gloria a Dios!*" (Glory to God).

Following the sermon, there may be "spiritual warfare," in which a designated leader will cast demons out of individuals or the congregation as a whole. Also, the highly publicized divine healing takes place, and scores of believers may line up in the front for prayer. There are also "testimonies" given throughout the meeting of answered prayer or divine power. Afterward, all shake hands, some chatting, others lingering for more prayer, as the crowd files out the door and back into the world. (For other descriptions of an evangélico meeting, see Gill 1990, Thornton 1981, Wilson and Clow 1981, Cox 1995.) In short, the experience is overwhelming to the senses, intimidating some newcomers and elating others. This is true even in small home meetings, which cannot boast of high-tech sound systems or awesome size.

Since evangelical meetings are strategically planned to draw in potential converts, it is not surprising that the impact felt after the first reunión can be profound enough to transform one's life. In the interviews, believers recalled a wide variety of strong attractions to the evangelical church.

The greatest appeal to those visiting an evangelical church are the worship, preaching, dancing, music, spiritual warfare, and healing that elicit participation, elation, and even awe from the congregation. Luís, a father of four who lives in a small shack on the highest point of the sloping barrio, witnessed spiritual warfare in a large church and never forgot it: "One Sunday I went and I saw the pastor cast a demon out of a boy, and as a Catholic this impacted me. I thought, 'I'm sinning.' I understood that the idols are things made by men. And I began to change in my way of thinking."

In evangelical churches, believers are encouraged to read and study the Bible in order to understand their experiences or lessons within the faith. This open, participatory style is appealing to many pre-converts who want "proof" or reason for the shared beliefs. (Thornton 1981:62). Also, the collective prayer is an appealing factor. Evangélicos pray to the divine as if they were engaged in a personal dialogue, expressing needs and sharing burdens with their "Father." The familiarity of their professed relationship with God is also evident in the language: in the barrio, the informal and intimate Spanish pronoun *tú* is used in prayer, yet the formal *usted* is used with all family members, friends, fellow believers, and neighbors. Therefore, God has exclusive intimacy through their language. This was the appealing factor for Diana:

> What they preach in the evangelical faith, they live. It's something real. In the Catholic faith, they don't teach the Word of God . . . they teach a person to pray and repeat the same prayer every day. They don't teach you that a dialogue with God is different. That's what I liked about the evangelical faith, what they preach, they live. All that they preach is to the foot of the letter in the Bible. It's not invented by man. Nor is it repeat, repeat, repeat like a priest does.

Believers also recalled a strong attraction to the worship and praise, which in Pentecostal churches is characteristically charged with emotion, loud music, and various mystical "manifestations" of the Holy Spirit. Carlos accompanied his wife to church to be sure that she wasn't lying about her newfound faith and cheating on him. He initially refused to enter. After waiting on the outside of the building for the length of a service several times, one day the music, clapping, and dancing heightened his curiosity and he went inside. Carlos so enjoyed participating in the worship that his conversion followed only a week later.

Individuals were also drawn by the "spiritual satisfaction" felt during the services. Loida, who runs a day-care center in her home, said, "The power of the Holy Spirit filled me, singing those beautiful songs. I would cry a lot. I felt peace, transported." Alberto's search had ended: "I found there what I had always been looking for. I didn't find it in another place."

The family-like atmosphere also was an alluring feature for many. Before and after meetings, believers greet one another, shake hands, hug, and chat. Pedro, who was a drug abuser when he visited the church the first time, liked "the harmony with which they received me. As soon as the meeting ended, *'Dios le bendiga, Dios le bendiga* (God bless you), We hope you come next week'. The unity. I saw that they wanted to bring me into their group." Monica also spoke at length about the warmth extended to her at the church where she converted:

> The treatment, the love, they loved us with a beautiful love. And they encouraged me. They would say, "We're going to pray for your home." And all the brothers would come, and pray, and ask God to help us continue and persevere ahead. They gave us examples of how to raise our children. . . . If we didn't have food, a brother would bring some. "Take this." Or if we needed something, "Take this." Or money. It was a beautiful love.

Evangélico churches make a point to love and welcome visitors as a conscious evangelistic strategy. Newell, a nineteenth-century evangelist, wrote, "[The newcomers] must be treated with such genuine cordiality that they will feel at once at home" (1882:108). In a violent metropolis such as Bogotá, where luxuries of physical safety, security, and trust are enjoyed by no one, the friendly warmth and greeting of the evangelical churches are a refreshing contrast.

Many times, I witnessed individuals in the midst of an acutely destructive situation receive sincere attention and care from evangélico churches. It came in the form of prayer, personal attention, or even monetary assistance. The experience would overwhelm them with deep emotion and gratitude, and their conversion would soon follow. For example, Jesica was living in conditions of dire poverty, struggling to keep her children fed while her husband lived in a drunken stupor. One day, after crying bitterly while she hand washed the laundry, Jesica was invited by her neighbor to one of the largest evangelical churches in Bogotá:

> So I went, and what I liked the most was that some brothers prayed for my home. They began to pray, like twenty brothers. And the pastor said, "Kneel here." So I knelt and they began to pray for the home of sister Jesica, that the Lord would take away the drunkenness. They began to rebuke the spirits of drunkenness. This impacted me—it's what most touched my heart. So when I left, I went with a tranquillity, a rest. And how all those prayed for my home, I felt important.

Another principal attraction of Pentecostal churches was the available pastoral care. Due to the shortage of Catholic priests in the barrio, pre-converts were surprised to get home visits, personal prayer, advice, and support. Mariela shared, "I liked how the pastor talked to us. I could tell him my problems." Latiana held a special affection for them. "[The pastors] worried about us. They don't worry about us in the Catholic religion. We really liked [the pastor]. He exhorted us with love, in the Word." Paternal relationships of instruction and guidance are established from the beginning of affiliation with an evangélico church. Within this persuasive environment, on the radio, or in any other situation of contact with a believer, the pre-convert may hear the message of salvation.

Hearing the Message of Salvation

The *evangelio,* or the gospel, is the creed that all have sinned and deserve death, but can gain eternal life through the crucifixion of Jesus by repenting and accepting Jesus as personal Lord and Savior. This is not unlike the doctrine of the Catholic Church, which also teaches Jesus' death as the redeeming sacrifice. Yet while Catholic beliefs are assumed true by their inherent place in Colombian culture, the Pentecostal doctrine is assumed true because it is taught and reinforced through heavy biblical instruction. Evangélicos not only want to believe in God and Jesus and the spiritual realm, they want to experience it all personally and deeply. They present the notion of an intimate relationship with God, an attractive element for spiritual "seekers."

True to their name, evangélicos broadcast the salvation message every way they can. One night, I accompanied Loida to go pray for a sick neighbor who was not an evangelical. She explained to the family that becoming an evangelical did not mean a change in religion, but simply a way to grow closer to God. After an evening service, zealous Alberto met young Sandro, whose ear had been slashed in a fight the night before. Alberto read several Bible verses and then said plainly, "You know, you might not be as lucky next time. Do you really want it to end this way?" He went on to describe how Sandro could find life and joy in Jesus Christ, and asked if he wanted to pray. María was in the psychiatric ward of a hospital when her sister came to talk to her about God. María remembers laughing wildly, but the words about salvation did not fall on deaf ears. Upon her release from the hospital, she sought membership in the evangelical faith.

La Caracas is a highly congested eight-lane bus route in downtown Bogotá, thick with sickening exhaust fumes. Homeless people sleep on the narrow grassy strips of the cement median, and garbage clutters the bus stops and lines the streets. It is a forbidding and threatening place, towered over by the skyscrapers of the city. On one side wall, beside fierce communist propaganda, there is a large sign painted with bright colors. It says, translated, "Are you tired of life? Christ in your heart gives you peace and love. Receive him today!" It stands out as a small yet constant reminder of hope from the evangelical community, visible to hundreds of thousands of bus passengers every day. Such evangelism takes place at work, at school, in one's home, in the street, over the radio, and within church meetings.

Sometimes, an individual hears the message of salvation but does not act on it immediately, for he or she has not yet been convinced of the Pentecostals' claims to divine power, personal peace, healing, and wholeness through God. Such a step is often made through an experience with the supernatural.

Experiencing the Supernatural

A supernatural experience is an event in which an individual encounters a force or phenomenon that cannot be explained by natural determinants. Every single believer in this study spoke of some miraculous event they had experienced, attributing it to God, Jesus, or the Holy Spirit. Occurrences such as healing, resurrection, spiritual encounters, divine protection, and supernatural provision were recounted with wonder. This is the conversion event that carried the most weight in convincing individuals of "the living reality of God." For a people without hope, resources, or power to combat desperate situations of emotional or physical frailty, the single awesome experience of feeling connected to a source of benevolent power was often the greatest reason to convert.

The most common experience was divine healing, as with Rosa. At the age of twenty-one (thirty years past), she acquired a terrible skin infection on her face. "It was like scabies," she said, recounting to me the burning itch it gave her. Dead skin constantly flaked from her face, and blood and pus oozed from the sores. She had to wear a silk handkerchief over her face when leaving the house. None of the doctors could explain what it was:

> I spent three months closed up in a room. My face was a monster. My eyes were so inflamed that they closed up. It was very serious. I was going to go see a witch, to see if someone had put a curse on me, but my brother, he was evangelical, took me to a meeting instead. He said, "The only one who can heal you is the Lord Jesus Christ."

That night in an Assemblies of God church, Rosa listened to an ex-priest from Spain share his testimony about how he found the truth of Jesus Christ through the faith of a young boy.

> So the priest said, "Those that want to be healed, come forward."
> I was the first to go forward. When that priest put his hand over me, I felt like I was flying. And I don't remember any more. I remember that I ended up on my bench crying and crying. There I received the salvation of my soul and the healing of my body. That night, I slept very well after three months of no sleep from this infection. I woke up the next day, and could see everything clearly. My face was not inflamed, and when I touched it, it felt so soft. My grandmother came in, and she said, "*Chinita!* What happened to you?" I looked in the mirror, and my face was clean. Clean! Totally well. And I said to my grandmother, "It was last night, the Lord healed me." From that moment, I have been in the ways of God.

Olga told the story about how her daughter was gravely ill, and even the doctors had given up any chance of survival. She entered an evangélico church in her barrio and asked the pastor to pray for the dying child. The next day, Olga's daughter had begun to recover. "The Lord healed her," said Olga. "This was grand for me. It made my faith grow a lot."

Patricia and her husband, Luís, still unconverted, had so little money that they sold many household items to feed themselves and their children. Finally, they had nothing left, and even less hope. A knock came on the door, and it was a young couple holding bags of groceries. "The Lord led us to your door," they said, and, leaving the food, they turned and walked away. Patricia and Luís live high upon a steep hill in the barrio, and at this time there were no identifying main roads, addresses, or telephones. "We were stunned," Luís told me, "and we sat in silence for a long time. We knew it had to be from God."

There are also supernatural experiences that were not related to immediate physical needs. During a time of despair and sadness, Luz went into a room to pray. The room filled with light, she told me, and a great voice spoke a Bible verse that filled her with encouragement. She felt then that God must be real. One day Eduardo had argued with his wife, and, feeling discouraged, he decided to attend a home prayer meeting.

> That day I felt sad in my heart. The devil was saying to me, "You had a disagreement with your wife, how can you be [praying] with

them, in this state? You're a hypocrite." Something inside of me wanted to be in that prayer, so I went. And I tell you the Lord had a great gift for my life. The Lord did something so extraordinary in me that all the weight—I felt a great weight on my shoulders, like I carried bags of stone—I felt that a hand took all that off me and I felt very light. The Lord transported me to places. That night, the Lord gave me very beautiful experiences, pleasant experiences, something that I won't forget. For me, from this point, my life began in the Lord. I believe he made me into a new being that night.

Such supernatural experiences draw an individual to the source from which they came. For the believers, they are evidence, proof that their God is real, actively working in their lives, caring for their personal needs (Clark 1958:195). Since the Pentecostal faith in Colombia is largely based on that which is unseen (the Holy Spirit, the presence of God, the blood of Jesus, and spiritual fulfillment), events that are felt by one of the five senses are unique and significant. Experienced in any stage of the conversion process, they are a powerful catalyst for personal faith.

As discussed in the "caterpillar" section of this chapter, nonevangelicals' perception of the faith is one of distant skepticism or mockery. For an individual to approach the evangelical faith with the smallest degree of openness, he or she must recognize a strong and acutely felt need for the salvation, miraculous power, or divine provision that the evangélicos claim to enjoy.

A common theme was expressed throughout the various stages in the path to conversion. Though each believer arrived at the faith through distinct circumstances, all were experiencing a physical or emotional need that impelled them to seek refuge within the church. The initial interest in the faith is often a survival strategy of sorts, a conclusion that is consistent with the literature discussed in the previous chapter.

Within this difficult situation or "crisis of presence" (Saunders 1995), the individual becomes more accepting of the beliefs and practices of the evangelical faith. He or she is willing to be prayed over and anointed with oil, to attend spiritually charged meetings, and even to listen to the Christian radio. This increased understanding of the evangelical faith and its fervent spiritual nature begins to transform the individual's worldview long before conversion ever takes place. What we see here are steps in a gradual progression of personal change that may take days or years. Since the decision to convert to

Pentecostalism has real consequences in the individual's life, it necessitates the assurance of time, consideration, and powerful personal experiences.

Liliana's story illustrates how personal need, compounded with elements of exposure to the faith, can be a strong incentive for conversion.

Fair-skinned, with gentle green eyes, Liliana was brought up as a Catholic in the capital city of Bogotá. Her father was violently abusive, forcing Liliana's mother to remove her from the turbulent home life and have her live with various relatives and friends all through childhood and adolescence. Although Liliana would fiercely defend the Catholic faith to anyone, in her bitterness she rejected faith in a benevolent God. "I knew of God," she recalled, "But to me he was a God of science fiction, so unreal, deaf to my prayers." Liliana was a harsh critic of the evangelicals, taunting their earnest devotion and prayers.

After a serious miscarriage early in her marriage, Liliana was told that she could never bear children. The news was devastating, for as an only child she had always longed for a large and loving family. When her evangelical landlord began to share with her about faith in Jesus, Liliana gave a mocking challenge. "I said to her, 'Look, Ma'am, if only this God of yours would give me one child, and soon, I'll convert to your religion with no questions asked and remain faithful forever.' You see," she laughed, "I didn't know that a powerful God existed, who would take this challenge." Undaunted by her contempt, the landlord returned with church elders, who prayed over Liliana. "The prayer they made did something in me," she recalled with sentiment. "Fifteen years later, I still haven't forgotten it. I felt such a joy, a peace that filled the room, an infinite rest."

Soon after, much to her joy, Liliana found that she was pregnant again. Although still critical of the evangélicos, she kept her promise and began to attend meetings. "As my belly grew, I started accepting them, listening, and being less rebellious. Something was drawing me to the faith." She soon converted and was baptized during her fifth month of pregnancy. Liliana went on to become one of the strongest members of her church and a mother of four children.

The resolution of a felt need through the evangelical church, together with a changed, favorable perception of the faith, often produces total religious conversion. The individual's worldview has been transformed to the extent that he or she views personal "surrender" to God as rational and desirable. Liliana affirmed, "I wanted to belong to the people of God." This was a considerable journey of change from her original loathing of the believers. Although every convert tells a different story, the shared theme is transformation within and without, over a course of time. One must remember that the affections of an individual are bound up in the heart, and it is no trifling matter to cast away one lifelong devotion in favor of another.

Predisposed by difficult circumstances, drawn by believers, intrigued by visits to the evangélico churches, guided to salvation by the believers' gospel, and inspired by supernatural experiences, certain individuals follow a progression of interest in the Pentecostal faith. It is a personal decision, lasting a moment or many months. If the individual believes that what may be gained through conversion is worthy of the sacrifice of commitment, he or she is led to repent and commit all to God.

The Moment of Surrender

The moment of surrender is the prayer in which an individual confesses his or her sin and rebellion against God, accepts Jesus Christ as Savior from certain death, and acknowledges God as supreme and sovereign Lord over his or her heart, soul, and life. The evangelicals call this moment *renacimiento* or becoming "born again." Experienced in a climax of desperation, or at the end of a long search, the moment of surrender is often profound, emotional, and life-changing. It is called *surrender* because the individual cannot retain the old lifestyle with its sinful desires and deeds if he or she wants to receive eternal life. The evangelicals in my study actually used the Spanish word *entregarse* (to surrender oneself) to refer to conversion instead of the word *convertirse* (to convert oneself). This step entails complete transference of loyalty, life purpose, and identity into the "family of God," signifying membership in the faith.

A conversion occurred during my return trip to Colombia in a small church in Nuevo Progreso. A woman stood at the front and repeated the prayer of confession and commitment to God, and the congregation prayed for her in soft voices during the conversion. "Turn around, now," instructed the pastor, when they had finished. "Look at all your brothers and sisters in Christ who are seated there." She did so, smiling quite bashfully. "Anything you need, in any difficult circumstance or moment of trial, come to us, for we are your family now and we will support you as our sister in God." The congregation erupted in applause and exclamations, and the woman was hugged and welcomed by the pastor. It was an emotionally charged moment.

Turner and Killian call this the "fusion of personal identity with the group identity" (1957:338). Thornton also recognized the energizing intensity of conversion in his study of Colombian Protestants: "This new fellowship provides the participant with identity, belonging, security, awe, and ecstasy, and a zeal to live his new lifestyle in spite of the difficulties to be faced as a religious minority" (1981:156).

In giving up the old identity with the "world," the convert is led to consciously shed the pain and problems associated with that world (Saunders 1995:334). As the convert steps into "new life" as a child of God, he or she may release years of pent-up pain, anguish, or suffering in a highly charged, emotional moment of tears. For this reason, the moment of conversion may be an experience of peace and light-heartedness. "The central [characteristic] is the loss of all the worry, the sense that all is ultimately well with one, the peace, the harmony, the *willingness to be*, even though outer conditions should remain the same" (James 1985:201, original italics). DeMaría confirmed this in his study of cults: "The conversion experience introduces a person to a state of joy and peace, certainty and love, confidence and energy unlike anything known before" (1978:108).

The fondness with which many believers recalled their conversion evidenced the intimacy and profundity of the moment. Loida experienced a liberating feeling in her conversion: "But when I went to the second meeting, I knew what purpose there was. And I received the Lord for the first time, and I surrendered all of my burdens to him. All that anguish I felt disappeared, and I didn't feel sad anymore . . . I had a best friend." Abraham recounted to me, "I perceived, I felt the great love that God has for his children in the evangelical faith, from when I began. I will never be able to change religions, it's very certain." Angela recalled her moment of conversion as "a personal encounter with God." Since many believers began their conversion process ridiculing evangelicals, living "hopelessly lost in vices," or enduring circumstances of extreme difficulty, they would reflect back during the interviews and marvel at the change they had experienced.

The Butterfly: A New Reason for Living

As discussed in the literature review and demonstrated throughout this chapter, potential converts are often initially drawn to the faith by the immediate solutions that Pentecostal churches offer for their pressing material or social needs. "I knew that I was going to find in that church what was lacking," recalled Ximena of her primary attraction. "It was a refuge, a place where people cared for me, loved me." Olga was drawn by her practical need for security: "At the beginning, the hermana told me that God puts a shield around you so that you're protected from danger. That was important for me, it was wonderful." When Marta's newborn daughter was healed of health complications after the prayer of some pastors, she began to believe, and her conversion shortly followed.

When considering the evangelical faith, the residents' focus is on acutely felt needs, not on philosophical or political issues. Living in an environment of insecurity, poverty, and hardship, the residents' life decisions are centered on keeping the most basic needs met. Not surprisingly, religious choice is often subject to this practical element. Almost every believer interviewed in this study was drawn to the evangelical faith by superficial interests that related to an unmet, pressing need in his or her life.

Therefore, the original interest in the faith is rather temporary, for such physical and emotional needs surge and ebb regularly in daily life. However, if the Pentecostal churches only offered practical solutions or hope during difficult moments, what would distinguish them from any other social institution, hospital, food kitchen, or counseling center? If this were the case, individuals would come and go rather sporadically as needs arose, without any reason to stay devoted over long periods of time. After the personal need has been met, why make a permanent decision of conversion and commitment to a faith that demands such sacrifice and devotion?

This is the point at which many scholars of Latin American Pentecostalism stop their inquiry—at the moment of conversion. Naturally, the conclusions they have drawn depict the faith as a great "Santa Claus" in believers' lives. Evangélicos have only to pay their dues, through meeting attendance and tithes, and social and material "benefits" will be available. Academics explain the success of this faith among the poor by pointing to the constant crises and daily struggles of the lower class, and how neatly the evangelical churches fill these needs. In essence, the believers' relationship to the faith is described as a mere exchange of goods and services, as though the church were a country club or a bank.

The shallow nature of this image is demonstrated once we go beyond conversion and into commitment. Long after the initial need or crisis has passed, believers are serving and worshiping with passion and devotion. Years after the elated moment of conversion, they are found evangelizing, leading home Bible studies, and serving as leaders in church meetings. Many believers hold fast to their faith long after it has ceased to make practical sense in their lives. Why is this? The answer to this question lies in the convert's new worldview. While the old worldview shared by Nuevo Progreso residents was focused on survival, the new evangélico worldview is focused on the individual's personal relationship with God. As discussed in Chapter 3, the prophet's servant caught view of an unseen fortress that would defend his people from certain death at the hands of the Aramian army. The servant's reasons for serving God would never be the same. In the same way, through worldview transformation, a radical change occurs between the convert's initial motivation for joining the faith and his or her new motivation for committing heart and life to it. The converts have not converted to a faith, but to a personal God. The butterfly now has a new reason for living.

As an individual becomes progressively interested in the evangelical faith, he or she is taught by the believers that all desirable things come from the person of God. Supernatural encounters, healing, provision, protection, joy, peace, love, and eternal life are believed to come straight from the divine, through any number of channels. The church introduces the new convert to a benevolent Father who desires a close relationship with his new "child." New believers are taught that it is God who requests change and commitment, and it is God who desires to bless and care for each person. There is no authoritative church hierarchy or mandatory ritual governing the convert's new faith, but a divine being whom he or she believes to be loving and powerful. This observation is crucial in understanding a believer's motivation for commitment to the faith. Consider Josué's affirmation:

> Through the word of God I know that only through Jesus Christ can a person find salvation. The Lord has given me life, and I want others to feel the way I do. I advise people, and I tell them things that the Lord has done for me. Looking at God, not man, not at the pastor because he preaches well. I keep believing because it's not the pastor who's going to save me, not a music leader, not the person who sings the prettiest. The person who saves me is Jesus Christ. Nothing can take me away from the love of God.

During evangelistic sermons, the preachers do not say, "We ask you to commit to the congregation and our belief system." They say instead, "God is calling to you to give your lives to Him." It is a person they speak of, not a cause, or creed, or particular group of people. "What an observer interprets as commitment to a set of beliefs or to an organization, a participant considers commitment to the person of Jesus Christ" (Gerlach and Hine 1970:100).

Angela gave a rousing sermon to her little congregation one evening. She taught that as much as believers enjoy singing and dancing at church, they need to understand that their very lives are to be a continual worship to God. Angela was attempting to deemphasize the "fun" of worship and focus the believers' eyes on God. A pastor in another little church proclaimed one Wednesday night, "To be a friend of God is the best we can be!" In a home meeting not a quarter-mile away, believers sat in a circle one Saturday evening and discussed how Jesus waits for them every day to come and talk to him, commune with him, share their hearts with him. Down the hill of the barrio, in a larger church, several dozen women sat in rows one Tuesday afternoon listening to the pastor teach:

> There are teachers, prophets, pastors. There are evangelists. But I believe that one of the first lessons that we should learn is to have a promise of direct love with the Lord. The ministries bless, but it's God who gives us life, who has given us salvation. And we have to learn to look to Jesus. The Bible says in Colossians, "Put your eyes on Jesus, the author and finisher of the faith." We are going to walk with God.

Conversion is the beginning of a "love relationship" with the divine. Ullman noted in her study of religious conversion, "What I initially considered primarily a change of ideology turned out to be more akin to a falling in love" (1989:xvi). Initially drawn by the social and material benefits of the church, converts then return seeking the intimate communion with God that collective worship offers. The spiritual intimacy and inner wholeness that they feel becomes the new source of passion for their sacrifice and service to the faith. The evangelical faith may indeed involve an exchange of sorts, but it is far more relevant, intimate, and spiritual than the material image that has been portrayed in scholarship.

The "personal relationship" is an important element to establish early in the study, for the reader will note as we progress through further chapters how this relationship with the divine is developed and maintained through church meetings and daily life. At this point, it has just begun. The moment of surrender is the end of the path to conversion, but the beginning of what is meant to be a lifelong endeavor. It is only the first step in the process of commitment to the evangelical faith, which now must be followed by real and symbolic acts of breaking away from the "world" and becoming immersed in the faith. We will study this aspect in the next chapter.

A young widowed pastor at the pulpit with her two children

5

"Learning to Walk in the Ways of the Lord": Commitment to the New Faith

No os conforméis a este siglo;	Be not conformed to this world;
Sino transformaos *por medio de la*	but be ye *transformed* by the
renovación de vuestro entendimiento,	renewing of your mind,
para que comprobéis cual sea la	that ye may prove what *is* that
buena voluntad de Dios,	good, acceptable, and perfect
agradable y perfecta.	will of God.

—*Romans 12:2*

For the new evangélico convert, identity with "the world and its sin" was buried in a moment of personal surrender to the lordship of God through the guidance of the church. Profound and life-changing as the experience may have been, it will be short-lived without the subsequent rooting and grounding effects of commitment steps. The path to conversion merely brought the individual to a place of open and willing acceptance of the Pentecostals' message of salvation. Now the convert is expected to enter into official status as a member and begin a life dedicated to the vision and beliefs of the church.

The steps of commitment can be defined as those acts and behavioral changes predetermined by the church that, when carried out, reflect the progressively deepening nature of a convert's devotion to his or her religious faith. Such acts of commitment are to be demonstrated both to the convert's new "family" of believers and to his or her nonbelieving friends, neighbors, relatives, and co-workers. These efforts force converts to break old ties with the "world" and give important meaning to new ties in the church. Social scientists and church leaders alike acknowledge that personal commitment steps are essential to the permanence and strength of the newly acquired belief (Turner and Killian 1957; Gerlach and Hine 1968:33; Thornton 1981).

73

As the new converts progress through the steps of commitment, two purposes are being accomplished. The first is that their worldviews continue to be transformed into the likeness of the evangelical faith. Biblical doctrine and church beliefs become the all-encompassing guide for interpreting daily events and making life choices. The second purpose is that as new converts sacrifice more of their lives to the faith and the church, their commitment is cemented and given high priority in daily life. It is important to remember that devotion and service to the faith are increasingly motivated by the developing "love relationship" with the divine that believers have.

The stage of religious change described in this chapter represents many crucial points of decision for the new converts. Public declaration of one's faith in an environment that is averse to the Pentecostal movement can be intimidating. Abandonment of traditional forms of entertainment such as secular music, alcohol, and dancing can be difficult for those whose lives were once centered on such activities. Learning submission and cooperation within the church family as one gives of precious time and resources is not without its frustrations, either.

Commonly, many new converts will decide that the costs of conversion are too high. They simply desert the faith and the congregation permanently or until another crisis emerges. Some manage to complete several stages of commitment and then fall away, afraid of backlash with nonevangelicals or having lost their motivation to belong to the faith. Few remain who have caught sight of something that seems priceless to them. These converts will embrace each commitment step with zeal, sincerity, and a willingness to give all for Christ.

Since the new converts' faith is young and unstable, the pressures from each side are acutely felt. Ties to the "world" are only recently broken, and nonevangelical friends and family beckon insistently for a return to the old lifestyle. On the other side, believers offer support and spiritual zeal, encouraging perseverance through the trials of new faith. Here the sincerity of the new converts' commitment to God and the church is tested, and only those who are sincere in motive and desire will continue on.

As in the path to conversion, individuals facing this stage of commitment will choose affiliation or not based on their own rational perception of the faith and its significance in their lives. Individuals and not exterior forces continue to be the central agents in determining personal belief and faith, though the rationale behind their decisions has now been influenced by the evangelical worldview.

This chapter will be guided by the two themes of worldview and relationship. I begin with a brief description of the biblical doctrine that transforms the converts' worldview and how this new interpretation of life explains their commitment. Then, five integral steps of commitment to the faith will be examined, using believers' accounts to describe the development of their relationship with God and the church. I close with a discussion of the evangelical worldview and how it changes the new converts' perception of their life struggles.

The Spiritual Realms

The Pentecostals in Nuevo Progreso share three basic principles of doctrine that are reflected in the shared worldview. A brief description of these will shed light on the rationale of their fervent behavior and religious practices.

First, Satan and God represent opposing spiritual realms that constantly battle over the souls of men and women. In the third chapter of the Gospel of John, Jesus frequently referred to this dichotomy, using incongruous terms such as "earthly" and "heavenly" (v. 12), "perish" and "life" (v. 16), and "darkness" and "light" (v. 21). In the minds of believers, a clear line exists between the two realms. Individuals are either part of one realm or the other, and such membership has eternal significance.

This dichotomy has been recognized in several scholarly studies of Latin American Pentecostalism (Burdick 1993:37; Mariz 1994:42; Cook 1985:227). "The basic conception is at once apparent. It rests on the dichotomy of the spiritual and the material, the church and the world, the spirit and the flesh" (Lalive d'Epinay 1969:108). This principle of opposing realms can be found frequently in the Bible, and its centrality in the Pentecostal faith is evident in songs, sermons, doctrines, and behavior.

Through the path to conversion and commitment, new converts begin to interpret all events and situations in their personal life and in the world as a manifestation of the conflict between the two realms. They see the widespread violence in Colombia as evidence of Satan's grip over the country, or as God's judgment for the sin that is prevalent. Prosperity and health are from God, and poverty and sickness from Satan. Drunkenness is caused by the oppression of a demon, and success is God's blessing. The Pentecostal belief system is all-encompassing, giving meaning to every aspect of the believers' lives. "These meanings illuminate for the individual the routine of everyday life and instill sense into the brute finality of life's crises" (Luckmann 1967:71). For new converts living amidst the irrational violence and perpetual hardship of Nuevo Progreso, this spiritual understanding of life is embraced as a source of purpose and hope.

The second principle is the belief that an individual lives in darkness, sin, and death under the influence of Satan's power until he or she crosses over into God's eternal life, light, and truth, an act made possible by Jesus' crucifixion. One must surrender identity with the "world," becoming "born again" in the family of God. As 1 Corinthians 5:17 says, "Therefore, if anyone is in Christ, he is a new creation; the old has gone, the new has come!" Rebirth is the key to Christian conversion, for as the bridge between the two realms, it separates believers from nonbelievers.

The terms used in this process of conversion, such as *death* and *life,* have a strong literal sense of finality and permanence, not allowing for mediocrity or fence-sitting. Indeed, evangélicos present the choice to follow Jesus as all or nothing. If an individual chooses to be a part of the Pentecostal community, he or she is expected to embrace all of the costs and responsibilities of the faith. There is no middle ground or casual mixing of faiths. The terminology of conversion that believers use is demonstrative of the serious nature of their commitment. They preach total commitment, and strive to live it.

The third principle held by the Pentecostal community is that believers are to be engaged in continuous battle as children of God against the forces of Satan. They must struggle against the "enemy" in their own lives and in the surrounding world, where Satan is busy destroying and killing. The world is like a drowning ship, and the believers' task is to bring Jesus' salvation to as many as possible before the end comes. Reflecting this belief, the Bible is full of verses that encourage believers to walk in strength and holiness in their daily fight.

Since the evangélicos view the world as a battleground, they feel individually responsible for fulfilling their responsibilities as soldiers. "In a revival of religion the soldiers of the cross strive to rescue prisoners from the enemy. It is a conflict with Satan over souls; it is a weighty, arduous business" (Newell 1882:198). There is an urgency in religious participation, as though lives and souls were depending on their prayer and faithfulness to God. They do not act as spectators, sitting passively in the pews. Rather, the believers view themselves as key players in the struggle, empowered to enact change and make a significant contribution in God's kingdom and in the entire world with their individual, humble lives.

The churches teach that each believer has special gifts that are needed to advance the gospel and strengthen the evangélico community. It is expected that members will participate with high levels of commitment, pressing on together toward their common goals. Demonstrated in churches all around Bogotá, fervent spiritual passion is the standard. Those who commit to the faith must be truly convinced of the reality of the opposing realms, and of God's personal interest in their lives, to give and serve with such devotion and fervor.

Commitment to God and the Church

What is commitment? Is it simply a pledge or promise to an obligation? Is it bound by a signature or a specific action? All around us, it is common to see many individuals making frequent and rather insincere commitments. An agreement to serve a client, pay a debt, fulfill a contract, or raise a child may or may not be carried out to the extent that was foreseen. Rapidly, signatures or verbal promises are losing value, demonstrated by the demand for collateral, advance payments, and prenuptial agreements. One's word is rarely trusted.

This same casual regard for commitment has reached the sacred domain of religious faith. No longer do believers consider the prayer of conversion to be an absolute binding pledge between the convert and the divine. Many individuals "pretend" to convert out of peer pressure, desperation, or as a means to meet a practical need. Therefore, the evidence for true conversion lies not in the moment of surrender but in the subsequent manifestation of the convert's inner transformation. As held in the secular realm, commitment is not the pledge but the fulfillment of that which was pledged. For this reason, this chapter will explore commitment as a visible demonstration of devotion to the purpose and vitality of a relationship over the course of time. Within the evangelical faith, the relationship is between the convert and God, manifested in personal life and in one's role within the church.

Due to the profound nature of commitment to the evangelical faith, it necessitates a gradual process of inner and outer transformation. Just as a recruit undergoes extensive mental and physical training in preparation to be a soldier, and just as an enamored couple passes through various stages of dating, courting, and betrothal, so the convert is given time and training to grow into his or her new evangélico identity.

Through extensive interviews and observation, I found that there were five general steps of commitment taken after the initial conversion. These steps bring a new convert into complete, recognized membership within the church. Though to an outsider they seem legalistic and even unnecessary, to evangelicals they are symbolic manifestations of "death" to the world and new "life" in Jesus Christ. The five steps are public testimony, bridge burning, indoctrination, conformity of behavior and appearance, and water baptism.

Although a believer's commitment can extend far beyond these initial steps, I will only examine these five in this chapter. They are the foundation that all believers share and the necessary prerequisites for further involvement or leadership. Contrasting the varied, unique experiences in the path to conversion, the commitment steps follow a more defined sequential order. Some may argue that "spirit baptism" must be included if I am referring to Pentecostals, but I found through my research that such an act only enhanced membership status and did not license it.

Testimony

Public testimony occurs when the convert testifies before the church congregation or a group of hermanos how he or she "arrived at the feet of Jesus" and received eternal salvation. Usually, it is accompanied by the actual story of conversion, complete with details about the previous life of sin, any important supernatural experiences, and the moment of personal surrender. This act accomplishes several purposes.

By publicly declaring one's new allegiance to God and the church, a convert becomes more convinced of the reality and significance of his or her own conversion. If the individual merely made the decision in a silent prayer during a service, he or she may question whether it was legitimate or final. Public testimony validates the conversion. Also, the heightened emotion of recounting events that led to surrender before an attentive and accepting audience gives converts a fervor for their newfound faith. The individual feels approval and importance and is eager to move on to the next step of commitment.

Newell's book *Revivals: How and When?* (1882) teaches the value of this practice: "I may add that testimony of young men for Christ is . . . a wonderful means of grace to themselves. It quickens, strengthens, and commits them to the cause. It is one of the prodigious forces by which *they are kept*. This practice should be continued" (p. 129, emphasis added). Gerlach and Hine also list testimony as a step of commitment: "Talking about a subjective experience effectively clarifies and reifies it for the individual and draws immediate reinforcement from the group" (1970:136). I witnessed several such events during the research:

Another person got up to give a testimony. She was of the world, she was in the hospital. Then she found Jesus and she's healed and happy and full of love and joy. We all applauded for her.

—*Field Notes*

Through the testimony, members of the church become aware of the individual's new status as a "brother" or "sister." Thus the new convert becomes subject to all aspects of membership in the faith: home visits, personal accountability, encouragement, discipline, and spiritual or material help in time of need. He or she is expected to submit to church authority, attend weekly meetings, and live according to the strict standards of moral conduct. Believers readily acknowledge that the first months after conversion are the most difficult in retaining one's faith, so a conscious effort will be made to encourage the new convert and keep him or her from "falling back into the world" (see Gerlach and Hine 1970:136). Testimony publicizes those new believers who will need this intense support and guidance.

Also, public testimony of salvation during a church meeting is a powerful influence of persuasion over those individuals in the congregation who have yet to convert. In the testimony, the new believer recounts his or her life circumstances before conversion, describing the doubt, anger, or pain that was acutely felt, and the nonevangelical may immediately relate to these emotions. Then, surrender is described as liberating, bringing joy and peace, and the visitor's own sentiments are triggered. He or she may begin to view conversion as the real answer, a solution, a life-giving decision. Testimonies by longtime members are also given in church meetings, as they may recount their conversion or simply tell of a recent miracle or answered prayer. Its effect is so stimulating on a congregation that all the churches in my study encouraged testimony in every church meeting. This will be explored in Chapter 6.

Bridge Burning

Burning bridges is the conscious act of severing the interdependence of intimate relationships with nonevangelicals in favor of following the faith. As 1 Corinthians 6:14 says, "Do not be yoked together with unbelievers." These old ties, which are said to hinder a new believer's growth, are then replaced by friendships within the church body (Gill 1990:713). Bridge burning is often a painful commitment step, one of the highest prices of joining the evangelical faith. In Thornton's study of Protestants in Colombia, 95 percent of the respondents agreed that a price had been paid in conversion, such as family alienation and isolation from friends (1981:81). The pastor of a successful church in Bogotá stated that it was almost necessary for a convert to break old ties and make a new set of friends (p. 82; Turner and Killian 1957:340). Berger described this in *The Sacred Canopy* (1967): "Thus he must disassociate himself from those individuals or groups that constituted the plausibility structure of his past religious reality, and associate himself all the more intensely and (if possible) exclusively with those who serve to maintain his new one" (p. 50).

Research shows that this step of commitment is highly enforced within deviant religious cults. The pressure from society against conversion to these groups is so great that converts must cut off all contacts to remain faithful (DeMaría 1978, Balch and Taylor 1977). In the barrio, however, converts were not required to leave their home or job, nor were they "cut off" from the world. They continued to work and live with nonevangelicals, but could not be influenced by the lifestyle and "sin" of those in the "world." Relationships that proved to be a deterrent to the convert's growth or permanence in the evangelical faith were to be severed. If that was not possible, as in the case of spouses, children, or co-workers, the believers were to utilize the intimacy of the relationship to "witness" and share about Jesus. Because the faith is evangelical by nature, contact with the world is encouraged and practiced.

Bridge burning sometimes occurred involuntarily, as some converts were simply abandoned by friends or relatives. Such was the case for Gloria, whose deep attraction to the evangelical faith ended her marriage. A mother of eight, Gloria's muscular physique and thick hands were evidence of decades of hard labor in the *campo*. She cried during the interview, recounting the suffering of her life before finding God. Gloria and her husband had just moved into a new house, and her new neighbors began to speak to her about the faith.

> One day they invited us to church. And I went with my husband, but he didn't like it at all. He strongly prohibited me from returning and said that I didn't have a right to go back there. But in my heart I was saying, "Yes, yes." I needed to follow Christ. I felt this hunger, this desire for the Lord. I wanted to go and kneel and make the decision. But I was afraid. My husband said not to go, detaining me strongly. But I went to several meetings anyway. They filled me, and I would leave with this joy. . . . I would forget all the problems, all that hurt me.

Several weeks of such conflict came to a climactic point when Gloria's husband left her for another woman. The lifelong tie was severed, and Gloria moved to Bogotá to begin a new life as an evangélica. She never regretted the decision to follow the faith: "I live happy with my Lord. I want to keep on with the Lord."

Eduardo faced similar heavy consequences for his new evangelical identity in a painful moment with his family. He and his wife Liliana were without money and desperately needed a place to stay:

> We were left without housing. So I went to [my mother's house] and I asked my mother to make a little space for us, a little room to live in, because we didn't have money to pay rent. She said, "I'll go talk to your father and your brothers, but in this house there's no room for you. And what's more, you've become evangelical. No, we're on *this side* . . . come tomorrow." So I went the next day and my brothers were there, together. They said to me, "There's no room here. But the truth is, you've become evangelical. You left our religion. The religion that our mother taught you since you were a boy, and taught all of us. So if you return to our religion, we'll find you a little room." And I said, "I'm not going back to that religion, even if I have to live wherever. I know God is not going to abandon me. Even if I can't come here anymore. It doesn't matter." So they said, "All right, if it's that way, there's no space for you."

Although the experience saddened Eduardo, he was grateful for an opportunity to show his family how serious his new faith was. He was also willing to pay the price of losing his family ties in favor of remaining faithful to what he considered was more important.

The new convert is instructed to abandon those relationships centered on activities deemed "sinful" by the Bible, such as heavy drinking, extramarital relations, and crime. Jorge was once an unyielding alcoholic, stumbling home drunk during the dangerous night hours of the barrio. He endured mocking criticism from his old drinking buddies when he converted to the faith. They teased Jorge, calling him "*fanático*" (fanatic) and "evangélico." Determined not to continue in his old ways, Jorge decided that he'd rather be called "evangélico" than "alcohólico." Although he used to drink every evening in a certain bar, after his conversion he did not return.

The believers were adamant that new converts should break ties with those friends who may draw a person "back into the world," for newfound faith is often weak. This was illustrated for me through the life of a young believer. Felipe, a twenty-year-old whom I came to know well, had used heavy drugs before his conversion. He even lived in the most dangerous streets of Bogotá for six months, witnessing untold horrors of death, violence, and poverty. Through a gradual time of change, he converted to the evangelical faith, and even enrolled in a strict rehabilitation center.

At the time I met Felipe, he was zealous for the faith, giving his testimony publicly in open-air evangelistic meetings, attending church and home meetings, and maintaining himself clean and sober. However, he continued to hang out with drug-abusing friends, claiming that he wanted to "witness" to them. The church leaders doubted Felipe's maturity and were not convinced that his faith could endure such temptation. They earnestly cautioned him that it would draw him back to the "desires of the flesh."

After a couple of months, Felipe began to lie to the believers, using their generosity to sustain renewed habits. By the time four months had passed, Felipe was completely back with the old crowd and involved in serious crime to fund his drug use. He began to sell his parents' valuables for drugs and exploded violently against his family members several times. He beat his younger brother and poured gasoline into the family's little food, breaking windows and wreaking havoc on the neighborhood. The police eventually became involved. A year later, the hermana who initially evangelized Felipe wrote telling me that he was living on the street again and looked horrible. She and other believers attributed Felipe's fall to his unbroken ties with the "world."

The book of 2 Corinthians says, "So from now on, we regard no one with a worldly point of view." The believer thus views himself or herself as a child of God who cannot be influenced by secular values. Now, one is a missionary, a witness to nonevangelical acquaintances so that they too can come to salvation. In Latin America, since one's social networks and family ties are often the key to physical survival, burning those bridges is a very powerful act of commitment to the evangelical faith.

Indoctrination

Indoctrination refers to the lengthy process of learning church doctrine, practice, and beliefs, and the corresponding Bible passages on which these are based. Since indoctrination begins before conversion and continues as long as an individual is part of the evangelical faith, it is not a single event. Nor does it demand high personal sacrifice, as does bridge burning. Indoctrination naturally occurs as one attends church, engages in corporate worship, studies the Palabra, and listens to Christian radio. By adhering oneself to the Bible, which is the fundamental basis of the religion, a new convert demonstrates commitment to and personal investment in the faith.

The prominence of the Bible is one of the most common characteristics of evangelical churches in Latin America. Upon conversion, believers in Nuevo Progreso purchased or were given their own personal Bible to study. Most church meetings begin with a Bible reading in which all members stand and read a chapter out loud, in unison. Believers attend several meetings a week, each of which include an hour of biblical teaching and preaching. All are encouraged to enroll in *instituto bíblico,* a formal Bible training lasting one to three years from which one earns a certificate. Literate and illiterate believers alike are able to quote key Bible verses for their daily situations, and they do so often.

Indoctrination, since it involves consistent and persuasive instruction of biblical principles, is the most powerful instrument in the transformation of one's worldview. The violence, unhappiness, marital infidelity, poverty, and suffering of barrio life are all given meaning through songs, Bible stories, and sermons. Verses and parables explain the deception of wealth, the value of hard work, the wiles of temptation, and the virtues of love, forgiveness, and generosity. Believers read about the violent warfare between God's kingdom and Satan's kingdom throughout the Old and New Testaments, and they begin to see daily life circumstances through the same perspective (Glock 1973:40). Gradually, mundane routines are infused with meaning and added significance (Snow and Machalek 1983:277). Believers, such as Jorge, often refer to this initial period of indoctrination as "eye-opening":

> I saw everything differently. It was like, in the world I had leather glasses and they had been taken off. I understood what is good and what is bad. And I took hold of the Palabra. At first, you think, "Those evangélicos, the pastor brainwashes them." But then one knows the Palabra more, because one is more instructed in the Holy Bible. One goes to the meetings, and the pastor gives the doctrine, the lessons. And one leaves there new, believing, having faith in God.

In Townsend's 1877 book *The Supernatural Factor in Religious Revivals,* he quotes a Mr. Emerson as saying, "Our eyes are holden that we cannot see things that stare us in the face, until the time arrives when the mind is ripened; then we behold them, and the time when we saw them not is like a dream" (p. 62). The believers often emphasized to me how they encountered this new perception of life that was made clear to them through indoctrination. Angela portrayed this with a song in her interview, taken from John 9:25. Translated, it says

> I am a witness to the power of God,
> For the miracle that he has done in me.
> I was blind, now I see the light
> The glorious light that Jesus gave me!

Through their "awakening" time, believers learn to ascribe a biblical interpretation to every situation or event in life. The evangélico vision brings all the events of the world under "God's plan," so that nothing is out of control or senseless. Even the atrocious Colombian violence, which has commenced a new field of study called *violentology*, is explained through indoctrination. Believers like Yenny gain a sense of peace and ease through such understanding:

> With everything that is happening around us, I see that the Palabra is being fulfilled. Everything is prophesied, I believe. So it's happening, down to the letter. The violence would worry me a lot before I came to the gospel. I lived in bitterness because of this. I thought about not having many children because they would suffer. I thought the world was going to end.
>
> Then I came to the Lord, and I learned the Bible. I learned many truths. The Lord opened my eyes perfectly, and I saw that things aren't what I thought they were. So I began to understand that all that had happened, and all that would happen, was the fulfillment of the Word.
>
> I used to live in this fear, I even dreamed of ugly things. Since I accepted the Lord, he has made this disappear in my heart. He gave me confidence, a faith, a trust that this wouldn't happen with my children. Wherever we go, the Lord protects us.

James (1985) also mentioned the "objective change which the world often appears to undergo" during the stage after conversion (p. 201).

In the previous chapter, we explored how individuals are initially attracted to the evangelical faith as they seek resolution for their pressing material or emotional needs. Through indoctrination, as their worldview continues to lose its focus upon daily survival and center upon an intimate relationship with the divine, this change begins to manifest in church meetings. It is an amazing sight to see women with modest attire and hands worn by years of manual labor, whose lives are burdened and stressful, come into a church service and weep in prayers of gratitude to God. They have begun to desire something intangible in the faith for which they would sacrifice all that they have in time, resources, and commitment. The believers begin to use phrases like "*mi Señor es tan lindo*" (my Lord is so beautiful) and "*Te adoro, amado mío*" (I adore you, my beloved). The perceived relationship with the divine becomes increasingly real for them, especially when the believers are taught to "see God" in all of the daily events and church activities. Personal faith acquires a self-perpetuating motivation. "Pentecostals will explain that Pentecostalism is not a movement or a belief or even a single experience. It is a *way of life* with Christ" (Gerlach and Hine 1970:197, original italics).

Indoctrination imbues the worldview of new converts with the values and beliefs of the faith. As the believers embrace this teaching, they become convinced of the rationale behind the moral standards that churches hold, including that of behavior and appearance.

Conformity

Conformity of behavior and appearance is personal submission to the strict norms of dress, appearance, moral conduct, and character that are enforced by the believer's church. Many Pentecostal churches in the United States were born out of the puritanical Holiness Movement of the nineteenth century, and in the transfer across cultures, much of the rigidity was retained.

In almost all of the Pentecostal churches I studied, for example, there were strict rules for a woman's appearance. They were to dress in modest styles of feminine clothing, with little makeup or jewelry, and long hair. Use of men's clothing was discouraged, as this did not glorify God. Once, as I sat in a small kitchen wearing overalls, boots, and a sweatshirt, having chin-length hair, I listened to a lengthy scolding from a believer who valued purity of appearance. My cultural difference would not exempt me from the biblical principles she revered.

Most women voluntarily changed their styles of dress through the commitment process. Surrounded with a church family who encouraged such modification, and filled with zeal to grow in holiness, the new converts made an easy transition. Alejandra recounted her own experience:

> God totally changed me. Also, God changed me in regards to
> makeup. I used to wear a lot of makeup—pencil, shadow, lipstick.
> One day I came home from a fast [at church], I looked at myself

in the mirror and saw that I looked very ugly. I said, "Lord, forgive me. I'll never put makeup on again." Just as he took the
makeup from me, he also took pants from me. Now, I don't use
pants, just dresses.

Alejandra's worldview had been transformed, and through this new
vision, old styles of appearance now seemed sinful. Her sister Olga
shared the same conviction to modify her image and behavior:

Before, I was wild. I liked the fiestas, I liked to wear a great deal
of makeup, with short, short hair. I never wore skirts, only pants.
And a little while after I arrived to God, he made me understand all that I should leave behind. I shouldn't wear makeup, I
shouldn't use pants, because the woman should dress like a
woman. And I give thanks to God for all he did with me.

Men were required to have short hair and to dress and behave
respectfully. Alberto, a young preacher, explained this to me once as
he combed his hair in preparation for a sermon. He said that an
evangélico should stand out for his clean and decent appearance,
drawing attention and respect, bringing new souls to Jesus. To carry a
Bible under one arm was even better. That summed up their belief:
whatever the "world" did, they would be different. The evangélicos
sought to stand out. By enduring the mocking gaze of neighbors or
fellow bus passengers, the believer was forced to defend the faith, or
negate it. Those with a strong zeal became more committed to the
cause of the group under such opposition.

Wife battering was absolutely forbidden, as was extramarital sexu-
al activity. Women were to honor their husbands and submit to them,
keeping the home and caring for the children, without engaging in
any form of gossip or passing time in the street. Men were to be sober,
responsible, loving fathers and husbands, providing for the family
and working for their children's future. I witnessed several sermons
in which the pastors strongly exhorted the men to reject destructive
macho behavior and live in harmony and humility.

This has been a topic of considerable scholarly interest (Brusco
1995, Gill 1990), for such religious norms have the potential to undo
abusive behaviors based in traditional gender roles. The evangelical
church has proven to be a powerful influence over behavior within
families, using personal accountability, group pressure, and spiritual
"warfare" to combat all "appearance of evil" (Colossians 3:5–8).
Married couples in my study listed "improvement in the home" first

among the changes they had experienced after conversion. This testifies both to the transforming strength of the evangelical faith and to the behavioral change that is expected during commitment.

Goldin and Metz best defined the modification of leaving "sinful" habits behind: "Specifically, conversion means a commitment to sobriety, to honesty, to monogamy, and to refrain from traditional celebrations" (1991:330). New converts were no longer allowed to attend worldly fiestas, nor could they drink, dance, flirt, listen to secular music, or watch secular movies. In a culture of festive parties and frequent celebration, this is a significant sacrifice. On the other hand, considering the demanding schedule of weekly Sunday school, worship services, evangelism, fasts, and prayer meetings, the believers have little time for worldly carousing. Finke and Stark observed that when secular activities are prohibited within a church, the only available alternative is religious participation. Therefore church meetings are anticipated, for they have become the believers' sole source of entertainment, expression, community, and fulfillment (1992:254).

One's relations with others were also expected to be transformed through conversion and commitment to Christ. Pastors teach believers to be holy, living examples of their faith so that others will be drawn to God. Carlos told me that he had the face of an ogre for his entire adult life. Neighbors were afraid to greet him, and his home environment was constantly destroyed by screaming, violent brawls. "After I arrived at Jesus' feet," he told me, "I began to smile and greet the neighbors, and my temperament was softened at home, at work, and in the street." No one could believe the change. Alberto was withdrawn and quiet with strangers, but with those who knew him, he was short-tempered and selfish. Now, his character had changed. He was eager to evangelize strangers and speak of his faith, and with friends and relatives he had become more gentle and soft-spoken.

Liliana often typed letters and résumés free of charge for her nonevangelical neighbors. Esperanza's model work habits and attitude at the club where she was employed earned her a good wage and the respect of her co-workers. At his construction jobs, Abraham would pray instead of responding angrily to condescending superiors. Marisol also experienced a change in character that affected her home and work environments:

> I was bad-tempered. I would yell and scream. I was furious all the time. I treated my children wrong. My husband and I treated each other badly also. There were screaming fights. There was no

peace between us. There wasn't the harmony and love that there is now. In my work, if I didn't like what they told me, gave me, I talked back. I was aggressive. I would throw things, and if I didn't want to do things, I wouldn't. I lived angry with my co-workers. We would fight. Now, no. In our house, there is the love of Christ, much peace, it's lovely. Also in my work, they know that I'm a Christian now. And now they respect me. They're not vulgar around me.

Conformance to the standards of appearance and behavior was required of all converts who expected to continue in good standing within the church. It demonstrated commitment to the faith in that it required high levels of personal discipline and sacrifice. Those who were not serious about their conversion were reluctant to give up vices and "ungodly" character traits, and their involvement often did not last beyond this stage of commitment.

The steps of commitment made up to this point have been informal stages that may occur as a brief, informal event or a process of several months. The final step of water baptism is a universally enforced ritual of commitment, deeply sacred to the believers, which marks the converts' official and binding entrance into the faith.

Water Baptism

Water baptism is a ceremony of public declaration of faith in Jesus Christ in which new converts are fully immersed under water by church leaders in the name of the Father, Son, and Holy Ghost. A period of indoctrination is required before water baptism, and the new convert must not be living in sinful habits at the time of the event. Depending on the church doctrine, the baptism may be symbolic of what takes place at conversion, or it may carry significant meaning for salvation, personal cleansing, or empowerment. For some, it represents the believer's burial, resurrection, and new life, imitating Christ's example.

Baptism is the sealing of the commitment of conversion, and for those hesitant about membership in the faith, it is the sacred point of no return. If we are speaking of the growing relationship between the believer and God, this commitment step holds a significance akin to the marriage ceremony.

Thornton also found that water baptism marked official entrance into a Protestant church (1981:109). In *El Bautismo en Agua: Un Baño Inútil?* (1994), a guide for Latin American evangelicals to understand the importance of water baptism, L. H. Gabriel affirms the common belief:

And in what manner will those who believe in Jesus be counted among his disciples? Nothing less than through baptism! As if baptism were the public testimony before the entire world through which [the converts] would show what commitment they had made and with whom! (p. 54, my translation)

Among the believers I studied, water baptism was such a significant event that it was mentioned only second to conversion as the biggest milestone in their Christian lives. Participation in communion (the sharing of bread and juice in commemoration of Christ's death), a common ritual, was only permitted to those who had been water baptized. Those who were living in *unión libre* (common-law marriage) were not allowed to be baptized until they had legitimately married within the evangelical church. Since baptism was a demonstration of a conscious choice to follow Christ, youth in the church could not be baptized until age ten or over, at which point they were considered ready to make an autonomous decision.

In late January 1996, I walked through several miles of dusty barrio streets with members of a church as they sang and played tambourines. We walked down the mountainside and to a rather contaminated river to witness the baptism of three believers.

Under the bridge they prepared for the baptism. Esteban stood with his hand out over the water, claiming it for God's glory and sanctifying it for the baptism. A couple of hermanos joined him. There were a small group of twelve or so believers on the bank, and three women dressed in white were waiting to be baptized. He asked them to listen, to look at the water, because downstream that way is going to flow the "old man"—the dancing, the liquor, the anger, the jealousy. The two younger girls winced at the abomination of the dancing.

"Why do you want to be baptized?" he asked them. "Because we are saved and we want to be," they answered. He asked them, "Do you believe in Jesus Christ?" And they agreed emphatically. "Well then, let's go . . ." He asked the first woman for her name and what she believed, and then using her full name, said, "I baptize you in the name of the Father, the Son, and the Holy Ghost." They let her hold her nose, and gave her a full immersion. Afterward, they clapped on the bank, and said "*Gloria a Dios.*" Someone started to sing, "Baptize me with your Spirit, Lord," and they all joined in, continuing for all three baptisms. Then Esteban stepped out of the water slowly, wet to his waist and shoulder, speaking in tongues.

—Field Notes

The significance of water baptism for the believers was the highest of all the commitment events. It could never be repeated, even though other rituals would (even conversion, for some). One's baptism date would remain fixed as the real beginning of new life. New converts claim that the effect of being immersed under water gives one a sense of gaining God's power to live in victory and perform supernatural miracles as Jesus did. It also brings personal change into one heightened emotional event. Jorge described his baptism:

> I made the decision [to convert]. So the pastor says, "You need to become baptized." So I went to be baptized, and everything changed for me. It was as if I had been tied up with wire, and then it was gone when I came up out of the water. One thinks at first, "All right, I'm going to take a bath there." No. It has power. And when I came out, I changed. Everything changed for me. The situation in my home, with my relatives, everything.

Even outside of the formal interview, Jorge loved to talk about his baptism. The enthusiasm and reverence that Pentecostal churches have for the event motivates young converts to embrace baptism and all of the commitment that it entails. It is a bittersweet celebration, for the "pleasures" of the world are no longer permitted after baptism. Yet, for the zealous new convert, no other incentive is necessary.

Same Struggle, New View

To summarize, the five steps of commitment to the evangelical faith are public testimony, bridge burning, indoctrination, conformity of behavior and appearance, and water baptism. Now, having completely converted and committed oneself to the evangelical faith, an individual has experienced radical changes of self and life. The old identity and ties have been lost, a new "family" has been gained, the mind has been saturated with doctrine and beliefs, baptism and communion have taken place, and character and lifestyle have been transformed.

The most fundamental change occurs within the believers' worldview, which is noticeable in their language, comportment, and interpretation of life circumstances. Before conversion, the worldview was to a great extent individualistic, borrowing from Richardson and Stewart's terminology (1977:24). Residents of Nuevo Progreso were forced to depend entirely on themselves for protection, provision, health, and general survival. They felt as vulnerable to attack as

Elisha's servant in the story described in Chapter 3. Although family networks are generally strong, the urban environment fragments these, and they cannot be relied upon. Through conversion to the Pentecostal faith, individuals acquire a collectivistic worldview, illustrated by Elisha's servant's vision of the great heavenly army. Believers become surrounded with an intimate network of spiritual and material support. Solutions, through faith in God, are believed to be readily available, for the churches profess that "with God, nothing is impossible." Diana's words exemplify the new mind-set of the believers in facing their daily struggles:

> There is a hope. In our daily life, there is a God who cares for us. We know that there's this Person in one's life. We can't see him, but we can feel him. He helps me to support my faith in him, to know that my life is saved. There's no need to worry about tomorrow, because he is there with me. Because the Word says that each day brings its own worry, no? And all has its time under heaven.

Originally struggling amidst meaningless difficulty, isolated by poverty and insecurity, they now feel part of a global family of Christians under an omnipotent, generous God. Once lacking in power and resources, they now believe they have direct access to the absolute source of power and provision. Difficulties do not disappear, but despair and worry no longer weigh down daily life. Julio, father of two boys, converted years after his wife did. He traveled extensively after the birth of their first son, and his lifestyle bore no responsibility for fatherhood or marriage:

> My life, before, was not ordered. It was empty. We had problems. And now that I know the Lord, you can feel this love and peace in the home. The things of the world passed, just like the Bible says. Now they are made new. My life has taken a turnaround. Also, my personal character has changed a lot. For example if one is without work, he becomes distressed, and angry. He treats the children wrong, and they live terrorized. But now, being in the Lord, one prays, and puts it all in God's hands, and we wait on him. And now, one doesn't worry, no matter how big the problem may be, one puts it in God's hands and the problem will be resolved. Although in the Christian life, there are many tribulations. But one can be calmer in dealing with them, because we know we have a powerful God that helps us and never abandons us. He's always with us.

A shared confidence is visible among the believers in the benevolence and personal care of the divine. This perception of God gives them a new way to cope with the difficulties of poverty and danger. It is a worldview that serves practical purposes in their lives, but the believers' devotion is not a means to a practical, material end. Their focus is God, and the believers cling to their faith in Him as the source for meeting any need. Loida expressed this same view: "I stopped feeling the difficulties. Everything began to change for me. Because the difficulties will always continue, but I had a faith in the Lord that somehow he would provide my food, my work. I didn't feel so afflicted anymore." Loida's steadfast trust in God's provision was her life buoy over the next several years during her husband's frequent, prolonged unemployment.

Does It End Here?

Here I have explored the process of conversion and commitment to the evangelical faith in Nuevo Progreso to demonstrate how the faith becomes such a strong reality in individual lives. The transformation is profound, touching every aspect of a convert's life and drawing him or her into a new identity, life purpose, and worldview. At this point, the converts have reached a place of stable, strengthened conviction, and are equipped to continue on as full-fledged believers. Have we reached the end of their story in the faith?

On the contrary. Official commitment may be sealed, but the believer's rugged, day-to-day commitment that must withstand hardship, discouragement, and fluctuating motivation has only begun. The transforming conversion process has provided a solid foundation on which evangélicos may stand and attest to the power and truth of their convictions. However, the zeal of conversion is often not sufficient to endure the daily struggles that working-class believers face. Their faith, like a tender plant, must be nourished, protected, reinforced, and encouraged. The true strength of the Latin American evangelical movement lies not in the conversion process but in the powerful "faith maintenance" practices that uphold the evangélicos' belief in the face of tremendous odds.

This concept of "faith maintenance" is a crucial key to the mysterious strength and influence of Latin American Pentecostalism. If the faith were composed of 60 million followers who all abandoned their newfound beliefs within the first year, it would be as feeble as sand clenched in a fist, falling away as nothing. Churches could not plan to buy big buildings with no promise of future income. The depth and sacrifice of commitment steps would be wasteful and even self-defeating. In essence, the Pentecostal movement never would have survived its first decade in Latin America. It would always have *converts,* and never *believers.*

How are believers strengthened and inspired to hold their faith high year after year? How is their intense commitment maintained under the challenging circumstances of daily survival? More importantly, how do churches maintain the believers' faith so as to elicit continued commitment and devotion? In the following chapter, we will explore the dynamic retainer of church fellowship and worship and its centrality in perpetuating the worldview of the believers.

Evangelicals in front of their hand-built miniature store

6

Staying *"Firme en el Señor"*: Faith Maintenance Through the Church

Mantengamos firme, sin fluctuar, Let us hold fast to the profession
la profesión de nuestra esperanza, of our faith without wavering, for
porque fiel es el que prometió. he who promised is faithful.
Y considerémonos unos a otros And let us consider one another to
para estimularnos al amor, y a provoke unto love and good works;
las buenas obras; Not forsaking the assembling of
No dejando de congregarnos, como ourselves together, as the manner
algunos tienen por costumbre, sino of some is, but exhorting one another,
exhortándonos; y tanto más, cuando and so much the more, as ye
veis que aquel día se acerca. see the day approaching.
—*Hebrews 10:23–25*

Soft-spoken with a gentle smile, Marta lived on the main street of Nuevo Progreso. She ran a *panadería* (bakery) on the first floor of her home and lived in a tiny, makeshift, two-room structure above the store. Her husband worked in the hot, stuffy back room of the bakery, making rolls, cookies, loaves, and pastries. At 7 A.M., she had already pulled up the huge rolling door facing the street, welcoming business from schoolchildren and day laborers.

Marta's job was a strenuous one. In addition to operating the cash register and supplying the display racks with fresh-baked goods, she stocked the walls with dry goods, soda pop, candy, and other foods. Customers would fill the picnic-style tables continuously, requesting to be served fresh coffee, tea, and bread. Marta swept the cement floor and wiped tables, received deliveries of supplies, aided her husband, and tended to the endless lines of those wanting milk, bread, soap, and chocolate. She rushed back and forth, taking an order from one person, filling a bag of bread for another, serving tea to a seated couple, giving change to a fourth. Her soft voice was heard saying,

95

"Yes, Ma'am, at your service. . . . Those are 100 pesos. . . . Two bags of milk?" All the while, there would be potatoes and meat cooking and snapping on the stove behind her for the family meal. Marta's work was punctuated by her children's needs of food, clothing, assistance with homework, supervision, and attention.

At nine o'clock at night, when most Nuevo Progreso residents had finished dinner and were preparing for bed, Marta was tending to the last few customers who needed milk, bread, or eggs for the family breakfast. When the shop closed, her work would continue. Her back was stooped with weariness by this hour, but such labors and long days were necessary to maintain her family and the bakery.

Sometimes, Marta would solicit a relative to tend the store while she hurried down the street to attend a meeting in an evangelical church. For she was a believer, and a faithful one, paying tithes, giving to needy members of the church, and participating in weekly meetings. She often cried during the music and worship, closing her eyes and lifting her hands. Her face had the expression of being lost in an encounter with a life-giving source. In her interview, Marta shared her conviction: "God is more than a friend. He's our everything."

Contrary to the romanticized ideals of religious conversion, believers' lives are not untroubled and carefree after they commit to the Pentecostal faith. In some ways they get worse. At every turn of the road there are ample reasons to abandon the faith. The environment of Bogotá is unsympathetic to evangélicos, sometimes openly hostile. The believers are consistently exposed to the "pleasures" of their old life, which beckon them to put aside strict religious convictions for a good time. The greatest challenge to the believers' faith is the struggle of daily life. When there is hunger, unemployment, or physical pain, it is easy to forgo trust in the divine and seek other help. Pressing needs demand immediate solutions, and the evangélico solution of prayer or fasting makes little practical sense. Furthermore, who has time for long meetings, or spare money for the church offering?

To the outsider who watches Marta and other evangelicals struggle under their heavy work and family burdens, the sacrifice made to remain faithful to the church "*no vale la pena*" (isn't worth the trouble). What could the evangélicos possibly be experiencing within the church that inspires their permanence in the faith? If an outsider views participation in the church as an added burden, what do the believers perceive it to be? Willems, in his research among Pentecostals in Brazil and Chile, marveled at the dedication of the believers: "After a full working day, more than five thousand had found time and energy to defy the distance and the unspeakable transportation system of a congested metropolis to attend an act of collective worship" (1967:151). How does the church help to encourage and maintain the fervor of the believer's faith in God?

To probe deeper into the strength of the evangelical movement, this chapter will examine "faith maintenance" through the church. We will begin with a description of a complete Pentecostal meeting as an orientation to the atmosphere of an evangelical church. Then, in order to provide meaning to the collective religious activity, the three fundamental elements of an evangelical meeting will be examined. Next I will look at the principal components of a meeting and their significance for personal faith, illustrating the discussion with field notes. Through this intimate view of church life, I hope to give the reader a clear understanding of how collective acts of worship perpetuate the believers' convictions and inspire their faith. As we explore the spiritual and religious experiences of congregations in this chapter, I also hope to provide an intimate view of the passion felt as believers engage in corporate worship to God.

A Wednesday Night Reunión

Buses were roaring up the steep hills, into the barrio, as weary laborers made their way through the dim, muddy streets and into homes. It was dusk, and the path to the church was only lit by bare bulbs hanging over the doorway of each silent home. I made my way, hopping over the open sewer ditch, avoiding heavy streams of rainwater, and speaking in soothing tones to the ever-terrorizing dogs. The deep throb of the electric guitar could already be heard several houses away as Esteban tuned it.

It was a Wednesday night meeting, and although it had not yet started, a dozen hermanos were kneeling on the cement floor, elbows perched on the wooden benches, praying aloud. Their voices rose and fell with emotion and meaning as they spoke in words of adoration and supplication to God.

After several minutes of this harmonic polyphony, Alberto greeted us with the common, "*Dios les bendiga, hermanos*" (God bless you, brothers and sisters). As if by cue, we rose from our kneeling positions with a responsive "Amen!" "I rejoice because you are here tonight," he said to us through the microphone. "But more importantly, I feel joy because the Lord is here. How many give thanks for the presence of the Lord? How many want the Holy Spirit to move in us tonight?" "Amen! Aleluya!" we shouted, accompanied by the resonating strum of the electric guitar. Behind the podium was a crude sign of hand-cut gold letters reading "*Santidad a Jehová*" (Holiness to Jehovah God).

There were about three dozen hermanos in the stark brick church. The women were in skirts and flat, muddy shoes, hair pulled back, wearing sweaters or coats to combat the chilly night air. The few men present were in slacks and shirts. One could sense the weariness of a long day of manual labor in the heavy droop of shoulders. Humble people worshiping in a humbler setting . . .

Alberto invited us to open our Bibles to Psalm 118, which we would read aloud together. He prefaced it with, "In the name of the Father, and the Son, and under the anointing of the Holy Spirit." Standing, we read the chapter, as Alberto led us with one verse and we followed with the next. At the end, he emphasized key verses and described their importance to our lives. First, in verse 6, the Lord is on our side—what can man do to us? "We have the victory in Christ, because he is our shield, our help, Jehovah God Almighty." "Amen," we responded. "Also, it says in verse 28 that we will praise God, and that's why we're here tonight, Amen? Brothers and sisters, we serve a living God, and he is worthy of our praise! How many believe it?" And we shouted our agreement.

The music started, and we sang a number of choruses of *adoración,* slow and reverent songs. The words to one went "How beautiful is the Lord, How lovely is my Lord. How beautiful is the Lord, today I want to adore him. The beauty of my Lord will never fade; the loveliness of my Lord will always shine." Another, "God is here, as certain as the air I breathe, as certain as the rising morning, so certain that when I sing to him, he can hear me. I can feel him, in the brother who is at my side. I can feel him, deep within my heart."

The believers stood singing, callused hands held high, eyes closed, some swaying back and forth. Alberto was leading us on the microphone in front of the church, while Esteban played the guitar. An hermana slowly swung a tambourine against her hip, her other hand reaching into the air above her. One hermano remained kneeling, his lips moving silently in prayer. A young mother beside me, her toddler on one hip, cried as she whispered prayers, "God, I love you, thank you Lord, thank you."

Although the music was not in harmony with the voices, although the loud twang of the guitar was distracting and even jarring, although kids squirmed and dogs wandered in from the street, the hermanos sang loudly, with gusto, almost shouting. Necks craned heavenward, faces strained from emotion. We sang the songs several times each, all from memory. There were no books, overhead projector, or any printed words. After each slow song there was a time for individual worship, in which people prayed to God and continued in personal words of adoration, while the electric guitar hummed out notes. "Your mercy is great, Oh God," prayed Alberto. "Let our lives be a worship to your holy name. Be exalted, beloved God, for you are great and merciful, aleluya."

When a half-hour of slow worship had passed, Alberto's wife Latiana went up to the microphone and cheered, "Who lives?" We responded, from practice, "Christ!" "And to his name!" she yelled. "Glory!" we yelled back. "And to his people!" "Victory!" "How many give glory to God tonight?" she cried, like a cheerleader during half-time. We exploded in applause and exclamations.

Latiana led us in forty minutes of *alabanza*, or upbeat praise. The guitar picked up a beat, several tambourines danced under expert hands, bodies moved, and hands clapped. We sang, "Oh dweller of Zion, praise Jehovah! Great are his wonders!" and "You have changed my sorrow to dancing, You have girded me with gladness! Only to you will I sing, my glory. Only to you will I dance, my glory!" The whole ambiance of the church felt as if it were springing to the beat, the kind that makes you want to jump, dance, laugh.

One song ended with the words to another, and tirelessly we shouted on. A little girl spun in the aisle. We repeated choruses again, and again, waving hands like victory flags, feeling the music move us and lift us. Several hermanos began to dance in their places, energized by the joy and vitality of the music. At the end of the alabanza, Latiana shouted, "To his name!" and we responded, "Glory!" and the electric guitar trilled and the tambourines shook and we gave a clap offering to God for a couple of minutes. "Aleluya!" shouted Esteban. "Praise be to the Lord!"

Believers found their seats, exhilarated, for it was time for announcements. "How many feel the presence of the Lord here?" pastor Esteban asked us, sweating from his vigorous guitar playing. "Amen!" we shouted, our fists in the air. He announced the meetings: "Friday night Bible instruction, bring a pencil and notebook. On Saturday morning there will be fasting from 9 to 12. The entire church should be here crying out for this barrio, for church growth, for spiritual cleansing. Saturday night, the Youth Meeting, but everyone should come, because we are all children in Christ, Amen? Sunday morning is Sunday School, for the whole family. Sunday afternoon, evangelism in the barrio, and Sunday evening at six, the evangelistic service. We'll have a guest speaker, and there will be much anointing from God with healing and miracles, so bring the unsaved to the feet of Christ, Amen? Home meetings are Monday night, and Tuesday afternoon, Ladies' Meeting here at the church. Amen, we're going to see spiritual and physical growth in this church. Aleluya, this church will see the glory of God."

An elderly hermana got up to pray for the tithes and offerings, and holding the little felt bag, she asked God to bless and multiply the money that would be given. While the offering was being passed, and coins dropped into the bag, pastor Esteban asked if there were any testimonies or music "specials." One group of young sisters went up and sang a song about not going to heaven until we've done the Lord's work. Their voices, delicate sopranos, together made one single voice as they stared at the ceiling and sang. We encouraged them through the song with "Amen" and "Gloria a Dios." Another hermano got up and sang with his old guitar a song about living for Christ every day. His face was worn and all but three teeth were missing, but we applauded at the sincerity of his music.

The young mother beside me went up to the microphone and gave a testimony of how God provided a job for her husband last week. "It's true that the Lord hears our cries," she said. We clapped. She was followed by handsome Gloria, who spoke in a soft voice of the back pain she had been experiencing. "The pastor laid hands on me in the last meeting," she testified, "And the pain left me! I give glory to God!" Someone trilled a tambourine as we clapped.

Then, the pastor asked hermano Carlos to lead us in prayer for the sermon. Just as we all sang at once, we all prayed at once, every believer crying out in his or her own words for God to speak to us, praying that our hearts would be open to the Palabra. The prayer ended, but we remained standing to read the Bible passage from which the sermon would be preached, to show reverence for the word of God.

Co-pastor Angela greeted the hermanos warmly as she opened her Bible. Her sermon was on the pool of Bethesda, a place in Jesus' time where the sick would go to receive healing. When an angel of God moved the waters, the first sick person to

touch the anointed waters would be healed. Pacing back and
forth all around the podium, she painted a grim picture of all the
sick lying by the pool, waiting for healing. She was an experienced orator, holding our attention captive for a complete hour.
Acting out the scene between Jesus and the paralyzed man whom
he healed, Angela extended her hand to the floor, and said,
"*Levántate, toma tu lecho, y anda*" (Get up, pick up your mat, and
walk). Again, shouting, "*Levántate! Toma tu lecho! Anda, en el nombre de Jesucristo de Nazarét*. The name of Jesus is power! Life!
Healing! Wholeness! Miracles!"

"Beloved brothers and sisters," preached Angela, when our
applause had died down, "How many hundreds of thousands of
people are out there sick, paralyzed, dying? We need to bring
them to the waters of life at Bethesda, so that God can perform
great miracles in their bodies! The water is the Holy Spirit
today—it always moves—and it is moved especially when we obey
God and want to do his will. We need to be a pool for these people! Preach, brother, preach! Draw the lost lambs to the healing
waters, to Jesus. Draw the sick, the abandoned, the lonely, the
afflicted, those who are paralyzed in spirit, and say to them,
'Levántate! Toma tu lecho, y anda.' How many believe in the
power of God? If we went out right now in the barrio, we'd find
people in need, waiting for healing, seeking help." She was com-
peting with the sound of a gas truck roaring up the barrio street
and distracted children, but she preached on.

"Do you want to be healed? That is the question Jesus asks
right now. Is Satan attacking you with trials and difficulties? Do
you have sickness? Jesus is here tonight, and he wants to make
you whole." Softening her voice, Angela then invited all those in
need of prayer to go forward. Over half of the congregation filed
to the front, filling the space in front of the podium, praying softly, hands folded or lifted, eyes closed.

As Angela softly sang, Esteban proceeded to each person and
asked his or her need. Then he would close his eyes and extend a
hand over the head of the hermano, praying and speaking in
tongues into the microphone. We who stayed standing in the
pews were encouraged to close our eyes, pray, extend our hands,
lift up our brother or sister to God. Esteban lifted his voice into
the microphone. "In the name of Jesus, I command the sickness
to flee from this body. I rebuke all power of Satan in this life and
this body, you are free, saved, in the name of Jesus Christ." The
brother fell backwards, limp, to the floor, cushioned by Angela's
arms.

The pastor moved on to the next hermana, anointed her infant's head with oil, and prayed for healing. The next hermano needed a job, so he could feed his children. The next hermana wanted prayer for her unfaithful husband. During this entire time, as Esteban spoke in tongues into the microphone, praying for wholeness and miracles in the name of Jesus, all of the brothers were praying aloud, fervently, hands extended, voices heightened with need, desperation, and supplication. The atmosphere was charged with a sense of encounter with the supernatural, that lives were changing, bodies healing, homes improving. "Receive the blessing, receive the healing," commanded Esteban, holding the gnarled hands of an elderly hermana.

Slowly, as they finished, those who had been prayed for moved back to their seats, some wiping tears from their eyes, others still murmuring prayers. "Gracias, Señor," prayed Esteban at the podium. "Brothers, give the Lord your heart tonight. Give him your life and ask him to fill you completely with the Holy Spirit, to renew your faith, to cleanse you of sin and unrighteousness, to show you his mercy and love. The waters are moving, brothers. Now is the moment for God to touch your heart and fill you with the strength and power of his Holy Spirit." With closed eyes we waited, whispering prayers. The young mother beside me had her hands up, as if to receive. "Pray, brothers and sisters. Let Jehovah flow through your spirit and soul." The hermano behind me said, "*Te adoramos, oh Dios, te amamos*" (We adore you, oh God, we love you), and I was very aware of a deep stirring sense throughout the room.

After a few more moments of silence, Esteban said, "Amen. There was much anointing here tonight, beloved hermanos." "Amen," we responded heartily. "God is so lovely, he has so much blessing for us. All we have to do is receive it." We sang one more song, only one time through: "Your faithfulness is great. Your faithfulness is uncomparable. No one like you, Blessed God. Great is your faithfulness." As the last notes faded, Esteban said, "May the Lord continue blessing you. We'll see each other on Friday night, for Bible instruction."

The meeting was over, and the hermanos milled around within the church for a few minutes to hug, shake hands, and greet one another. Eventually we headed out into the dark chilly night of the barrio toward home, walking in groups. The meeting had lasted over two and a half hours, and at this time of night, no one should be walking alone in the barrio.

It was almost symbolic, the contrast between the lighted

warmth of the one-room church and the muddy, dim streets of the barrio with lurking shadows and vicious dogs. As I found my way around the worst of the mud, I could hear the fading voices of some hermanos as they continued to sing into the night.

—*Field Notes*

Elements of Church Life

There is no greater stimulant for one's faith than participation in a collective act of worship among a congregation of fervent believers. The atmosphere is charged with enthusiasm, spirituality, and unifying strength, which uplifts the discouraged and satisfies the hungry soul. Durkheim recognized the centrality of the congregation in *Elementary Forms of Religious Life* (1915): "In all history, we do not find a single religion without a Church" (p. 59). It is within the church that the worldview is taught and reinforced. There, each believer is important as part of the powerful whole, as a soldier in an army. Though the Pentecostal identity may elicit ostracism or contempt outside the church, within the family of believers this identity is celebrated and embraced. Church meetings stir up and encourage personal faith in God, for when persons with the same beliefs come together, there is heightened awareness of the source of their passion. Simply stated, there is power in collectivity.

Through observation of the dynamics in Pentecostal meetings, I found that there are three fundamental objectives accomplished through the consistent congregating of believers. Every ritual or activity that the believers engage in within the church plays a direct role in fulfilling one or more of the three purposes.

The first of these is the *vertical* objective, which relates to the personal relationship between the believer and the divine. During an evangelical meeting, a sacred environment is created through collective prayer and worship that gives the believers a strong sense of proximity to God. Since intimacy with the divine is a fundamental objective in the faith, the church's role as a channel or facilitator for such communication is essential.

Called the "house of God," the church is revered by the evangélicos as a special, holy place, free of the distractions of the world, where God manifests himself to each individual and ministers to him or her in a close and personal way. Within the church, believers feel free to cry out and express themselves openly to God about any particular situation they are facing. The evangélicos hold fast to the belief that God hears their prayers and will actively respond.

Believers claim to sense God's "presence" in a special way through the practices or rituals of a meeting. In turn, they sing to the divine, pray, worship, and express their devotion to him, without the usual interference of home or work life. By creating an environment conducive to personal "communion" with God, the churches are encouraging believers to actively renew their own faith. As believers pray in their own words to God, expressing thoughts and desires, the sense of having a direct, uninhibited channel to the divine is reinforced. The vertical purpose of church meetings powerfully invigorates the believer's perception of and trust in a close and caring God.

The second purpose is *horizontal*. By congregating together and engaging in collective acts of worship and biblical instruction, the believers reinforce their unity as one church family. They are able to meet the social and material needs of the members in the congregation because each person contributes time, resources, and money for this purpose. Each plays a crucial part in the functioning of the whole.

When dozens or thousands of believers join together, a powerful spiritual fervor is generated in worship and prayer that solitary devotion cannot equal. There is a sense of supernatural power, of divine encounter, as though the passion of the whole is far greater than the combined sum of individual devotion.

For example, the sound of hundreds of voices lifted in soulful adoration is deeply moving, for it creates a great symphony of emotion and heartfelt belief toward God. I witnessed several congregations engage in spiritual warfare, all with hands extended toward the visible or invisible "battlefield," all stomping and shouting in forceful and authoritative tones, claiming the blood of Jesus and the power of the name of Jesus. Through the highly charged spirituality of this experience, it is difficult not to believe in divine benevolence, or that a demonic realm exists that daily comes to battle with God's people.

When fasting believers come together to kneel and pray, pleading for "unsaved" lives and the deliverance of Colombia, there is no mistaking the urgency in their voices. The responsibility that they feel to intercede for people dying in sin is momentous. Surrounded with the desperation of many prayers, one feels compelled to kneel and join them in the struggle, regardless of personal beliefs. Even sociologist Christian Lalive d'Epinay, in his research among Pentecostals in Chile, was stirred in his observations of worship: "I am sure that, had I been a Chilean peasant or labourer, I would have been caught up by the power of this collective contagion, of which I have felt the impact" (1969:xxiii).

Believers' relationships with one another directly influence personal commitment to the faith. They hold one another accountable to faithful church attendance, acceptable moral conduct, and personal spiritual growth. Yina expressed appreciation for this mutual support: "In my church, they don't laugh at you with your problems. They say, 'We're going to pray for you, tell me what you need.' They try to be with us. And in each difficulty they say, 'Don't dismay, the Lord is with you, he is your strength, keep on in Christ.'" The gifts of each hermano are valued without regard to education, appearance, or background, encouraging high contribution and participation. Through Sunday school, testimonies, music, home meetings, evangelistic activities, and church maintenance, all have an opportunity to serve and interact with others, strengthening their sense of worth and their bonds with fellow believers.

In *The Sacred Canopy* (1967), Berger recognizes the strength in religious collectivity: "The identification of the individual with all others with whom he significantly interacts makes for a merging of his being with theirs. [This identification] is carried in his blood and he cannot deny it unless he denies his own being" (p. 60). Many believers in my study considered their church family to be closer than their real family, for the worldview and life purpose they shared created greater bonds of belonging and support.

The third major purpose achieved through church meetings is *evangelistic*. Believers are equipped with the knowledge, confidence, and know-how to actively proselytize family members, friends, coworkers, or even strangers and bring them to the church to "meet Christ." This is not necessarily an explicit part of the church meeting, as are prayer and worship. However, through the collective acts of spiritual cleansing, biblical instruction, and divine infilling, the believers feel empowered to be "lights of the world," "witnesses," and "messengers of peace" for the lost and hurting, much like angels at the pool of Bethesda.

During services, the believers also receive encouragement and fortitude to continue sharing their Christian faith in spite of rejection or persecution. "Every active member is not just a churchgoer but a missionary who does not recoil from the ridicule and contempt which the public may heap on him" (Willems 1967:218). In this sense, sermons often take on the appearance of a half-time, locker room pep talk, reflecting the evangelistic purpose of the believers' lives outside the church.

The vertical, horizontal, and evangelistic purposes of religious congregational activity complement one another naturally much like the balance of the three dimensions (length, width, and depth).

When one is lacking, the church seems rather "flat." The presence of all three is necessary, for each has a distinct part in fulfilling the fundamental objectives of the evangelical faith. These are to love God, to love brothers in the faith, and to reach the world with the message of salvation. Churches that provide healthy mediums through which to accomplish these objectives are essentially allowing believers to carry out the lifelong assignment given to them during indoctrination. Practiced regularly, the vertical, horizontal, and evangelistic purposes stimulate believers' convictions and reinforce the pillars of their worldview.

Components of a Meeting

In Chapter 3, I discussed how existing studies portray the Pentecostal movement in Latin America as a cash machine of sorts where believers may make free withdrawals for their social and material needs. Also described as the Santa Claus image, this view holds that believers only need to "be good" with tithes, attendance, and Bible study, and the faith in turn offers them various social and spiritual "goodies" or benefits. The focus of this perception is essentially upon what the believers gain and receive, as if that were their sole motivation for membership in the faith.

Many academics who have observed Pentecostal church activity are distracted by the poverty and hardship of believers' lives and are quick to assume that the faith fills a practical, desperately needed role for them:

> One may say that Pentecostalism is, on the one hand, the *expression* of real misery, and on the other hand, a *protest* against real misery. It is the sigh of a creature who has been overwhelmed, the feeling of a heartless world, as well as the spirit of an age deprived of spirit. (Lalive d'Epinay 1969:35)

Rituals and practices within the church are viewed by many scholars through a lens tinted by the belief that the believers' lives of suffering are like a great void, with nothing to give and everything to receive.

The greatest weakness in this viewpoint can be found in the believers' participation within their congregation. It is true that congregational activity offers a needed escape, release, catharsis, and renewal to the participants. The evangélicos themselves will readily admit that. Yet attaining these benefits is not the focus of the worship, prayer, and teaching. The benefits are instead a byproduct of the greater purpose that is being carried out, which is the believers' active expression of devotion, thanksgiving, obedience, and service to God. To be loyal in examining the motivation for church participation through the believers' own perspective, we must recognize that they do what they do not necessarily to receive but to give, to be ministers unto God, to offer gifts of praise and prayer, and to serve their savior, provider, and friend. Through this, their faith is renewed and their spirits lifted. In this section, as we examine the components of a meeting and the content thereof, this concept will become increasingly clear.

The Power of Prayer

Prayer is designed to be a prolonged personal dialogue with the divine, in confession, adoration, intercession, or supplication. It is practiced individually, before the service and during worship, and also corporately, as the believers pray together for a specific, unified purpose.

Evangélico churches encourage believers to engage in prayer before every service. Members arrive ten minutes to a half-hour early and kneel, bow their heads, and pray out loud. Many lack the privacy to pray for an extended amount of time in their own homes, and the church is for them a sanctuary of open communication with the divine. The evangelicals believe that through precursory prayer, individual believers can be cleansed of sin and worldliness in preparation for the meeting, thus allowing for closer communion with God and richer spiritual blessing during the service. Also, they pray for the meeting, that God's presence would be there, that God would be glorified, that he would speak his Word to their hearts, and that the worship would bless God. In essence, through this prayer the believers are taking an active role in the success of the meeting by preparing themselves to be responsive, open, and "holy" vessels for the divine presence.

The following was taken from a recording of a young leader's prayers before one meeting. Transcribed, his prayer filled over ten pages. Here is a short excerpt:

> This morning, Lord, we come together with the purpose to worship and bless you, to glorify you and exalt your greatness, because your Word says, "Great are your wonders," and your mercies are new every morning, Lord. Therefore we worship you. We glorify your name, Oh God, Rose of Sharon, Lily of the Valley, because you are precious, Lord, because you are beautiful,

Father. This morning, be Lord over every life. We pray believing that where two or three come together in your name, there you will be, Lord. This morning we are asking that the blessing be over each one of us, that the windows of heaven be open. Permit us this morning to be adorers in spirit and truth. Take away this morning any weight of iniquity or weight of sin, all sin. This morning we kneel in your presence, we humble our lives before you, so that you can forgive the wickedness of each one of us. Send out what is not of you.

In his famous lectures, William James stated, "Prayer is religion in act; that is, prayer is real religion" (1985:366). Believers are able to enter into the mind-set of worship and repentance during the prayer before a service. They also utilize the time to make special requests to God for those in need. Angela was engaged in such intercessory prayer one evening when I arrived at the church:

> Wednesday January 17th—I entered at 7:00 sharp. Already, Angela was praying into the microphone, on her knees with her elbows on a bench, crying out to God. I saw Roxana on her stomach by the podium, praying as well, resting her torso on the podium. Many hermanos were already on their knees, praying. Angela, speaking into the microphone, prayed for the meeting. That God's presence would descend on us tonight, that God be glorified, that the Holy Spirit fill this place, we want to worship and adore you, Lord.
>
> She began to pray for an hermana, that God would touch her heart, that he would lift her, heal her, and she prayed for the situation she was in. She also prayed for a man, and all the things he needed. She came to a point in the prayer that she was audibly crying and raising her voice to pray for these people. Other voices in the church—soft, strong, full of emotion, all at once so mixed that it seems like a hum, a low symphony.
>
> —*Field Notes*

Precursory prayer sets a fervent tone for the rest of the meeting.

The believers hold fast to the biblical promise from James 5:16b: "The prayer of a righteous man is powerful and effective." Their pleading and adoring words are not spoken as empty rituals or obligatory phrases. Though thousands may be praying simultaneously, they believe that God hears and desires each individual prayer. Requests are made in expectation of an answer, of a fulfilled promise, of God's manifested goodness. Olga said, "The search for God is through prayer. You find him through prayer."

Corporate prayer occurs at intervals during the reunión. Believers pray collectively for the church, community, nation, neighbors, nonevangelical relatives, and the "unsaved" of the entire world. Prayer is offered before a Bible reading, asking that God would speak to their hearts, and afterwards, thanking God for the gift of his Word. Tithes and offerings are prayed over, that God would multiply the money and resources for his purposes and glory.

The believers lift up the pastor in prayer, that he or she would speak the word of God during the sermon. After the sermon, there is corporate prayer to send out demons, to heal the sick, to perform miracles in individuals' lives, and to help strengthen members of the church who are in difficult circumstances. By expressing their needs aloud to the congregation, individuals open doors of emotional support and even material solution from their brothers and sisters in the faith. Corporate prayer has practical and spiritual functions.

During church fasts, I have witnessed prayer that continues for two or three hours, everyone speaking aloud, kneeling or standing, crying out to God. At the single spoken word of a church leader or pastor, the entire congregation began praying in loud, fervent tones for whatever needs were expressed, as in this meeting:

> She invited us to pray with her for the meeting. The people are almost trained for this. It is quiet in the church as the leader talks, then he or she lifts a hand and closes his or her eyes and suddenly everyone in the church does the same, praying aloud, like a river had suddenly rushed into the room with all its roar and might. The prayer goes on like this for two minutes or so, and then you can hear, "In the name of Jesus," and the sound softening, and quietness, then the lady inviting us to say "Gloria a Dios" again.
>
> —*Field Notes*

Individuals in the evangelical faith believe that they are spiritual channels through which the presence and power of the divine may flow. They see prayer as the arduous yet exhilarating lever that opens this channel and brings about miracles and supernatural transformations. The gathering of believers all in desperate prayer gives a participant the sensation of expectancy, of power, of partaking in something mysterious and great. This was evidenced in the shared belief of Elisabet's church that their continuous prayers were literally holding up the country of Colombia and postponing certain disaster.

The actual word for fervent prayer that the Colombians use is *clamar*, the translation of which is "to cry out, to clamor," expressing the passionate nature of their dialogue with the divine.

Reading the Bible

Collective Bible reading at the official beginning of the church meeting is a common act held in reverence by all evangélico churches. It reinforces the evangelicals' belief that the Bible is divinely inspired and is to be continually used as a guide for all spiritual instruction and daily living. Corporate Bible reading also draws the believers together in a unified activity at the beginning of the meeting, bringing to a close the individual prayer that goes on beforehand. All members participate, which gathers in those believers who are still chatting, arriving, or finding a seat. The theme of the selected text of the Bible also preludes further prayer, worship, or even the sermon later on. Leaders point out key verses to remind the hermanos of the purpose of coming to church and engaging in worship to God.

In collective Bible reading, believers are affirming their allegiance to the shared beliefs of the faith. "[The beliefs] are not merely received individually by all the members of the group; they are something belonging to the group, and they make its unity. The individuals which compose it feel themselves united to each other by the simple fact that they have a common faith" (Durkheim 1915:59).

The Worship Service

Worship is perhaps the most popular activity within the evangelical churches. The Latin culture loves music and dance, and this is evident in the shared enjoyment of worship in Pentecostal meetings. One always finds at least a couple of tambourines in an evangelical church in Bogotá. Larger churches often have five to six hermanos playing as a complete band on an elevated podium. There are always worship leaders, who may be accompanied by up to ten backup singers, all on microphones.

A popular practice is to have a dance team, made up of young men and women who swirl and dance in choreographed motion to every song, fast or slow. Sometimes, scarves or flags are used for further effect. Within the smaller churches, the tambourine is the common instrument, often played with amazing skill and dexterity. As Harvey Cox observed, "Most Pentecostals gladly welcome any instrument you can blow, pluck, bow, bang, scrape, or rattle in the praise of God" (1995:142).

Music is an ageless medium that expresses the emotions and passions of the human heart (Cook 1985:119). It inspires patriotic loyalty, arouses sentiments of love, hate, pain, or triumph, and lifts the spirits of the weary and burdened. Within the Pentecostal churches, the worship is largely comprised of Bible passages sung to music, or biblical themes in contemporary language. It is a powerful stimulant for one's faith, for as the believer sings about God's beauty, might, and holiness, his or her perception of a caring, personal God is reinforced. As the believer sings about the chains of death being broken by Jesus' love, his or her gratitude is restored and deepened. As the congregation dances and claps to choruses of victory, joy, and strength, there is a sense that no difficulty or suffering will be impossible to bear. The revivalist preacher William Newell wrote of the power of music in 1882: "Sacred music is an almost indispensable factor in revivals of religion. It deeply imprints upon the soul the sentiment of the words sung. True music is heart-warming" (p. 250). Consider the words to this popular evangelical song in Colombia:

> Christ breaks the chains, Christ breaks the chains
> Christ breaks the chains, and gives us security
> How is it possible to live without my Jesus?
> You are the foundation of my life
> You freed me from hell and death
> How is it possible to live without my Jesus?

This is another favorite that conveys the revitalizing role of music:

> Renew me, Lord Jesus
> I don't want to be the same anymore
> Renew me, Lord Jesus
> Put your heart in me
> For all that is within me needs to be changed, Lord
> For all that is within me needs more of you.

Adoración is the name given to music with a slow beat, which generally expresses praise to the divine for his manifested faithfulness and love. It also conveys the gratefulness and sacrificial offering of one's life and heart back to God. *Alabanza* is upbeat and lively, usually accompanied by clapping, dancing, and spirited music. In both forms, the believers respond and move to the music, openly communicating feelings of sorrow, joy, adoration, and gratitude. "Pentecostal music provided ample opportunity for such emotional release. Every particle of their being was poured into worship as they sang" (Nichol 1966:64–65). I remember being startled at the expression of some men during the adoración in a larger church:

> There were three slow songs—each one sung many times, lasting ten minutes each. The pastor was playing the electric keyboard

and had a microphone, and a woman sang. The dancers in the front—dressed in sashes and white dresses—moved their arms slowly and gracefully in unison with the music. The people of the church responded naturally to the songs, raising their hands, closing their eyes, singing loudly and with meaning as the song was repeated. I noticed that there were more men who were emotionally expressive in the service than women—men who shook their arms with passion, who raised their hands, who faced the wall, whose bodies moved with the music, whose faces winced and grimaced and searched as they sang. It is quite a contrast to the Latin man I find in my daily life here in Colombia.

—Field Notes

At times during worship, several members will stop singing and just pray, cry, or even wail. The atmosphere of the church during such times is charged with emotion and is especially moving. Once I observed several women who seemed lost in their own supplications to God:

All of the songs were fast paced, and everyone was clapping. Songs of victory over problems, songs of joy to serve the Lord, songs of what kind of God we have. It went on for a good forty minutes, and we were clapping the entire time. Some people had their hands up and eyes closed. Each song was sung six to eight times. . . .

I saw several people really get into the worship—the men were even more expressive than the women, moving more, clapping their hands over their heads. As we sat down after the last song, when announcements started, there were still four women with their hands up, crying, singing, praising God. The emotion on their faces and in their gestures was so intense that it brought tears to my eyes. But they weren't stared at or hushed—they were accepted as everyone else, part of worship.

One woman wasn't finished when the worship ended, and instead of gradually sitting down like the other three women, she turned and got on her knees in sobs, crying out to God—"The Lord be praised"—in a raspy voice choked with emotion.

—Field Notes

In an average meeting, worship lasts forty-five minutes to an hour. During one vigil I attended in a small church, we sang for over three hours straight. Faulty sound systems or old instruments did not discourage the Pentecostals in my study—their capacity to sing seemed interminable, and they enjoyed it immensely. While they sang and praised God for salvation, provision, healing, faithfulness, and love, their reasons for belonging to the faith were reinforced and their motivation renewed.

Carlos was employed as a delivery man for a magazine company when I met him. He spent over sixty hours a week in the congested, heavily polluted, seemingly lawless traffic of downtown Bogotá on a motorcycle. "At the end of the week," he told me, "when I worship in the church, all the tension and bitterness is lifted." Melisa viewed adoración as a direct channel to the divine. "It seems to me like a divine chorus, it transports me and I feel closer to God. There are moments when one can feel very close to God." Patricia expressed a passionate side of worship: "When you get into the Lord, when you feel the power of God and it takes hold of you and you cry and cry. You begin to sing only for the Lord, and all else is forgotten."

The Tithe

Tithing is a highly encouraged practice within the evangelical faith in which believers give 10 percent of their wages to the church. The believers are taught to give cheerfully and generously in gratitude for God's goodness and blessings. In return, they believe that God will multiply their resources and provide for all of their needs. As hermanos invest with precious money and resources, they take a personal interest in the affairs of the church, and desire its vitality and success.

A principle is reinforced within the church that states that if a person tithes first to God, then there will always be enough money for other needs. At first, Julio told me, it was difficult for him to believe that by giving away his money, he would prosper. He had labored for every peso his whole life, and couldn't imagine tithing a full 10 percent to the church: "I would think, 'I can spend this money on something else, on bills, things more important.' It was an obligation. But little by little I've seen the blessings and benefits of tithing and of the Christian life. I've come to tithe out of love, responding to God. . . . The Christian life is good."

When I interviewed Marta, I asked what she would do if the food and money ran out. Who would she turn to? We were sitting on crates in a tiny room above the bakery she ran. She thought about it for a few moments, and then responded, "The Lord has taught me one thing—to tithe. If I'm lacking in the tithe, I lack many things, and many things happen to me. That's why it's pleasing to tithe. I know that God will bless me, and I won't lack food. They've taught me this in the church since I converted."

"The practice of tithing—giving a tenth of one's income to the Lord's work—is taken seriously by all types of Pentecostals" (Gerlach and Hine 1970:51). I often heard pastors conveying the importance of tithing to the believers, as in this sermon:

> What we have is from God, no? Sometimes we're ungrateful when we have to minister to God. Solomon offered the biggest offering to God, the most abundant. For months, there were mountains of offerings! If we'd do the same thing, this nation would prosper. We are priests, we should sacrifice to the Lord. It doesn't matter if you earn 10,000 or 50,000 pesos—the percentage is the same, 10 percent. What's important is not quantity but faithfulness to God.

In one meeting, the pastors thought of a creative way to collect the tithe:

> We took the offering, having a prayer first, and playing catchy music. We had to walk up row by row, dancing to the music. Esteban played as Angela sang, because "the Lord wants cheerful givers." People were laughing, falling over each other, running into each other and dancing in the aisles as they gave their offering.
>
> —*Field Notes*

In spite of their poverty, the believers were generous to their churches (see also Lalive d'Epinay 1969:54; Mariz 1994:72), sharing with the pastors a vision of growth and blessing for the congregation.

Giving Testimony

Testimonies are personal stories, given by members of the church, of God's provision, healing power, protective care, or salvation. When believers perceive the power of God in difficult circumstances, they are encouraged to share it with the entire congregation. This gives other members real-life examples of the manifest presence of the divine in their midst, stimulating them to continue believing in the faith. Newell witnessed the same effect in his congregation in the late nineteenth century:

> One man or more rises in a praying assembly to beg the prayers of God's people, or to announce a new hope in Jesus, and this is sometimes done with such spiritual emotion that the whole assembly is electrified. . . . Near the close of a large meeting the next evening I called for testimony. Instantly he rose and spoke earnestly of his new experience. The effect was prodigious. No

sermon that I ever preached began to equal it. (1882:123–124)

In small home meetings, testimonies were simple stories of divine miracles in day-to-day living, shared within the intimacy of a dozen or so hermanos. Sometimes the leader asked everyone to share, and other times the believers voluntarily offered testimonies of special, supernatural experiences. We heard of such things as extended work deadlines, safe childbirth, free food or clothing, safety from danger at night:

> We sat down and it was time for testimony. The woman leader praised the Lord. Her little son had climbed up to a wall of loose bricks, and they began to topple. But someone, a worker, saw him right on time and grabbed him out of the way, and she knows it was angels. . . .
> Ximena gave a testimony that she was glad the Lord had blessed her with the store and kept her safe, and wanted prayer for José who was sick. Diana gave thanks because God knows our needs and helped her buy a gas stove and other needed items. Mariana wanted to give thanks because God had helped them with their debts. Carlota gave thanks because she had finished her first quarter in school well and had received a good grade on a recent test.
>
> —*Field Notes*

Whenever someone shared a testimony, all others would rejoice with an "Amen" or "Gloria a Dios."

In larger churches, the testimonies shared were more sensational and less spontaneous. Pastors recounted miracles of awesome significance that brought enthusiastic applause from the congregation, reminding them that "nothing is impossible with God":

> Then the pastor got up and greeted us. How many have come for healing today? "Amen!" We shouted. He called a woman to go to the front. "How many recognize her? No one, because she's only been going to this church for ten days." He told us the story of how she was in a wheelchair eight days ago. (She had walked to the podium. Applause.) She had an operation and was in a wheelchair—and didn't think she'd walk again. Then she came to a meeting, in which he explained how one needs to have faith, and what faith is. He made the prayer of faith and told her to get up and walk. And she did.

To demonstrate, in front of everyone, he had her move her
legs and lift her knees. There was more applause. "And we give all
the glory to God," he said.

—*Field Notes*

The practice of sharing real experiences with God's power was
important in maintaining the morale of the believers. It gave them
ways to find eternal significance in all positive events of their lives,
therefore reinforcing the shared belief in divine goodness. Since
many facets of the faith are unseen (God, Jesus, eternal life, hell, and
heaven), believing has an element of risk. Testimonies bring the
intangible into the tangible, providing "proof" for the evangélicos
that the God they cling to is actively caring for each individual.

Preaching

Preaching is a universal practice in Christian churches that Pentecostals have embellished into a dynamic, captivating rendition. In
Bogotá, the sermon holds the same importance as worship, taking
forty-five minutes to an hour, half of the church meeting. It is no
petty task, for the believers have high expectations of the content and
delivery of the *mensaje* (message).

The congregation prays for the preacher before the sermon,
extending their hands out toward him or her, that God would speak
in an "anointed word." Sometimes they are fasting to increase the
power of the message. Believers listen with open ears and hearts,
trained to revere the pastor's words as the voice of God himself.
Aware of the congregation's needs and challenges, the pastor must
deliver a sermon that invigorates the believers, strengthens their faith
and commitment, teaches them biblical principles, fills them with a
desire to evangelize and share, and exhorts them to live holy and fervent lives before the Lord. The believers expect to be spoken to stern-
ly and to see manifestations of God's power through the pastor's
words and actions.

Elisabet's pastor had one of the largest churches in Bogotá, boast-
ing a membership of thirty thousand believers with round-the-
clock prayer and fasting, 365 days a year. She had great respect for
him:

I don't know another person like him. . . . He lives in the Spirit,
he's guided by the Lord and not by the people. There are pastors
who are afraid to exhort people because then the people might
leave the church. But that's like a bad father who doesn't teach
his child right, so afterwards there are bad consequences. Glory

to God that he corrects us. He is a man with a lot of love and humility. The Lord directs him. All the time he's sending out demons, of course.

"A good Pentecostal preacher is worth hearing, for he has a genius for communication; his preaching is not a lecture but a dialogue. The speaker challenges his followers, and asks for their approval" (Lalive d'Epinay 1969:53). Throughout the sermon, the preachers in my study would engage in an exchange of sorts with the congregation, encouraging their participation and stimulating their attention. They would say randomly, "*A Su nombre!*" (To His name), and the people would respond, immediately, "Gloria!" After an important declaration of a biblical principle, the pastors would ask, "*Cuántos lo creen?*" (How many believe it?) and the congregation would boom out, "Amen!" The pastor would recite the first half of a well-known Bible verse, and the believers would finish it. He would state a crucial doctrinal truth, and then have the congregation repeat it. The people were experienced at responding physically and verbally to a good sermon, and rarely could one find a quiet congregation.

By drawing the believers into the sermon, the pastor was encouraging their Bible knowledge and spiritual understanding. By participating in the sermon and giving approval to it, the believers were demonstrating their willingness to obey the Bible's commands and participate in the shared vision of the church. Their dialogue reinforced the common desire to follow Christ and gave a strong sense of teamwork in accomplishing the difficult mission before them.

The pastors used Bible stories, personal testimonies, real-life anecdotes, jokes, and riveting quotes to illustrate their sermons. Their words brought to life, at close encounter, the mysterious, invisible realms of God and Satan, causing believers to either shudder or respond with gusto in their seats. Consider these sermon excerpts:

> "There are many spiritual beings ready to attack us. If we don't prepare ourselves, we'll be destroyed. Our fight is not against flesh and blood, but against principalities and powers. We have to arm ourselves with the power of the Holy Spirit and the knowledge of the word of God. Before leaving the house, we should have a battle in prayer! God is ready to support us, protect us."

> "What is your definition of God? What does it mean to you? Friend? Father? God is a King, and we as his sons are kings as well. God spoke the universe into existence with a word of life—and in the same way, we have life in our words. But we need to believe and not have fear, and recognize our authority that as

believers we have power over life and death and healing. The
angels obey us."

—*Field Notes*

The pastors of the churches in my study considered the members
of their church to be their spiritual children. The training and discipline of their children was a serious task, heavy with eternal responsibility. During the sermon, the pastors had the complete attention of
the believers, and usually packed it with instruction of how to maintain oneself *"firme en el Señor"* (firm in the Lord) and not to fall away
into the destruction of sin and rebellion. At the end of the sermon,
he or she would challenge the believers to a new level of faith in God,
leading them through prayer, spiritual purging, and renewal.
Empowered, refreshed, their commitment renewed, the believers
would leave feeling ready to face the world again.

Healing the Sick

Personal ministry is a popular, publicized practice that involves giving
one-on-one attention to individuals for their physical ailments and
other prayer requests. While the "waters are being stirred" within the
congregation, as Angela described earlier in this chapter, those sick,
afflicted, and suffering hermanos are invited to partake in the divine
gift of physical and spiritual wholeness. It is a tender moment to witness a pastor praying over the heartfelt needs of individual believers.
Many endure difficult circumstances with very little encouragement
or personal support, and the caring attention given by the church
during this time of prayer often moves individuals to tears. Physical
sickness is a common occurrence in the marginalized barrios of the
city, and medicine and doctors visits strain the few resources that the
believers have. Through their ministry of divine healing and personal
prayer, the churches are meeting the specific, pressing needs of
believers or "seekers." By seeking spiritual solutions, evangelicals are
demonstrating their belief that God is the answer for everything—
even for practical, day-to-day needs and challenges.

In the larger churches, it is impossible to personally pray for each
of the hundreds who come to the meeting sick or afflicted. In these
services, the entire congregation is led in a prayer of healing, in
which the believers basically lay hands on themselves or their neighbor and ask God to intercede supernaturally and restore their bodies.
Afterwards, the pastors encourage the hermanos to move and stretch
the part of their body that was hurting them to confirm the healing.
This is followed by applause and exclamations of gratitude to the
divine.

When a believer experiences a miracle in his or her own body or life, that event becomes a touchstone of inspiration. Esteban proudly recounted to me several occasions of divine healing that occurred through his ministry as a pastor:

> One time, there were old women in the church, and their hands and feet were twisted and gnarled. They could hardly walk to church, and couldn't serve in the congregation. We washed their feet in a service, and after that they began to work again, dance, and worship the Lord.

After one Sunday morning service, Latiana carried her baby son up to Esteban for a special ministry of healing. A lump had begun to grow near the baby's eye, and she was worried. The pastor prayed, said Latiana, "and put a drop of oil on the baby's eye. The next day he was all well."

At a women's meeting one Tuesday afternoon, an hermana went to the microphone and began to cry, expressing a felt burden for the women with nonevangelical husbands. She called these women up to the front to be prayed over, saying that their struggle was a bitter one. Two dozen hermanas poured out of the aisles and knelt at the front as several spiritual leaders laid hands on them and prayed. The church began to echo with the mingled sound of strong praying, soft weeping, and earnest supplication. Several of the leaders had once been in these women's shoes and were now imparting the strength and encouragement they knew was needed.

The personal attention given to those in difficult situations of physical or emotional need generates bonds of love and support among believers. Many feel that they have been touched by God himself through other hermanos during this special ministry time, inspiring their belief in the empowering hope of the faith.

Spiritual Warfare

Spiritual warfare is actively engaging in the invisible conflict between God's and Satan's realms, which is manifested in a number of extraordinary behaviors within the church. Pentecostals believe that anyone may be oppressed by a demon or evil spirits. They practice *liberación* (deliverance) from such evil spirits, sending out greed, lust, infidelity, idolatry, drunkenness, violence, or any other sin from afflicted persons.

Sometimes during a meeting, church leaders will identify individuals within the congregation that need to be "freed from Satan's control." Other times, people voluntarily ask for deliverance, believing that it has power to solve a specific problem. The pastor or leader then prays and speaks in tongues, often shouting, as they command the evil spirit to leave the person by the authority of the name of Jesus. This is a sensational event, for sometimes those individuals being "delivered" fall to the ground, thrash, wail, speak in strange voices, or engage in other violent behavior. Some do nothing, standing, head bowed, as the prayer takes place. Members of the church take part in the purging ritual. Extending their hands, they pray and cast out demons as well, speaking in tongues and saying "*Salga, fuera!*" (Get out!) in forceful voices. As believers progress in the faith, they grow in the confidence of their ability to wage war against the unseen realm of Satan.

One evening I arrived at Angela and Esteban's little home to accompany them to the midweek meeting. I was immediately met by several extended family members who fearfully recounted to me their struggle with a demon-possessed boy the night before. The boy had thrashed about wildly on the floor for a couple of hours, unable to be controlled by others. The demon had spoken in a gutteral voice through the boy of its dominion over his soul, threatening to end the boy's life by midnight that very night. Believers wrestled in prayer around him, oblivious to all but the momentous task of delivering the boy from demon possession. Later, Angela arrived, and exerted her spiritual authority to send the demon away. When all had settled, the boy was limp, but the believers felt victorious.

Spiritual warfare is a strong maintenance factor, for as believers battle in prayer against the perceived evil realm of Satan, their loyalty to the cause of the evangelical faith is intensified. In their worldview, the demons are everywhere, plotting to draw the believers away from the evangelical faith, oppressing those outside the faith, and causing suffering and death. The harsh contrast between God's kingdom and Satan's realm that is reinforced in the churches instills a fear in the believers' hearts of falling away from God. They cling to the church community and seek to be fervently committed to God at every moment, so as to not fall from the faith. As Hebrews 2:1 says: "We must pay more careful attention, therefore, to what we have heard, so that we do not drift away."

A Date with God

In the previous chapter, I discussed how the believers' motivation for membership in the church changes during the commitment process. Often, they are initially drawn to the church by personal need, but then remain in the faith because of their new relationship with the divine. In the interviews, when I asked individual evangélicos to explain why they belonged to their particular church, less than 5 percent mentioned any sort of material "benefits." They pointed to the biblical teaching, the worship, the love of the brothers, the felt presence of God, the spiritual power, and the continuous prayer and fasting. They liked the functions of the church that heightened their sense of intimacy with the divine, because that had become the believers' central motivation.

For this reason, in spite of the costs of membership in the faith, the evangelicals did not perceive participation in the church as a burdensome task but as an anticipated event. They viewed their relationship with God as a treasure that held the highest importance in their lives. Since their faith was inspired by the endless *bondad* (goodness) of God, the believers gave generously of their time and resources to the church.

The personal relationship with God gained such significance in the believers' lives that they would leave a church if they didn't sense God's presence manifested through rituals and other hermanos. Some even recounted leaving churches with high material benefits in search of ones with *sana doctrina* (sound doctrine) or stronger faith. Such was the strength of their conviction that believers wanted their churches to help them maintain their personal faith. They were convinced of the power, reality, and eternal significance of God's kingdom and Satan's evil realm, and believed that without unceasing vigilance and care, they might fall away.

Angela had a powerful reminder on her wall. Translated, it read, "If Jesus Christ is God and died for me, then no sacrifice will be too great for me to do for him." She and her husband were pastors of two churches, a task that demanded attendance at twelve weekly meetings in addition to home visits, emergencies within the congregation, hospital visits, and hours of planning and music rehearsal. They lived with their four children in a tiny two-room makeshift house that had a roof of plastic sheets held up by wooden poles. Her life was a sacrifice, yet she preached to the congregations, "*Vale la pena seguir a Cristo*" (It's worth the trouble to follow Christ).

For Angela, the church was her source of life, for it was the visible, palpable, living representation of all God's invisible, mysterious, powerful realm. Alberto, a young father, was drawn to his congregation every week for two reasons:

> It's a place where I can take all my problems, difficulties, and I
> have the security that when I come out, I come out calm, without

problems, trusting in God. I find the support that you can't find in people. Also, there I find God. This means a lot. A church without God is nothing. But when I go there, it's like I have a date with someone, an encounter with someone—who will favor me, or help me, or do something with me.

Julio was unable to attend midweek meetings because of his work schedule. He considered the Sunday school meeting very important and anticipated it:

The love and peace that one feels, being in the church, it attracts you. You miss it, you want Sunday school to come. You miss it. You want to seek God. If I don't find time to seek him, knowing all that he gives to me, providing, giving life and health. To not respond to him for all this would be very sad. I tell my family, you can't just believe in him. You have to demonstrate it to him. How? By going to the church, glorifying and adoring him. Every day I need to seek the Lord. If I don't go, the rest of the week I remember I didn't go . . . I *need* to go.

Melisa was raised in the evangelical faith from birth. Now, married with young children, she sewed at home to keep a steady income. Melisa was encouraged during church meetings to continue believing in God, for they refreshed her trust in the divine's perceived care and faithfulness:

Sometimes one falls behind in the faith, away from God. But after being in a service, in which you can pray tranquilly and communicate directly with God, one understands, and leaves the church more willing, encouraged, knowing that God is definitely there and he hasn't abandoned us. He always thinks of us as very important. As minimal as we are, little in any situation, we are big before God because he is with us to strengthen us in any way.

The prevailing theme among these personal examples is that the Pentecostal movement in Latin America is not necessarily made up of converts, but of believers. Their participation in a collective act of worship is not generally motivated by material needs or social anomie, but by a true desire to have a personal encounter with God, whom they regard as living, benevolent, and personal. For the majority of believers, their experience within the evangelical faith has been so real and convincing that they desire to transform their lives, take on a new identity, and embrace the sacrifice of commitment to the church and its mission.

Staying Connected

Collective acts of worship that elicit high participation from individual believers are powerful, inspiring experiences. Through the rituals of worship, prayer, and biblical instruction, the beliefs of the congregation are emphasized and reiterated. The meetings confirm for the believers their conviction in the reality of God's kingdom and Satan's realm, and in the importance of individual holiness for the spiritual "battle" they must face every day. The meetings are designed to encourage the hermanos, invigorate their faith, and equip them to face the struggles of work, family, and barrio life. Through the power of congregational worship, the worldview of the believers is collectively produced and reinforced on a regular basis. Their commitment to God and the faith is maintained as church attendance provides spiritual "food" for the believers' lifelong journey.

When confronted with situations that challenge personal faith and force one to choose between obedience to God and association with the "world," a believer's decision often depends on the strength of his or her convictions in the Pentecostal faith. If one's belief in the reality of God has been recently reinforced by a rousing church meeting, the chances of falling away are much smaller. Participation in congregational worship is absolutely central to maintaining one's personal faith.

Does this mean that personal faith is only stimulated within the church? By no means. In light of the strong personal nature of the believers' faith, it is clear that commitment is hardly dependent on the functions of the congregation. For sometimes churches fail to meet the believers' needs, or they divide or fall. In spite of this, the believers continue on, supported by the strength of their own convictions. To understand this intimate element of personal faith, we must examine the believers within the context of their daily struggle with poverty, violence, and hardship. That is where the hard-core maintenance must take place.

An evangelical—who has lived in the barrio since its earliest stages—with her granddaughter

7

"My God Will Never Abandon Me": Faith Maintenance in Daily Life

Por cuanto en mí ha puesto su
amor, Yo también lo libraré. Lo
pondré en alto, por cuanto ha
conocido mi nombre. Me invocará,
y yo le responderé;
Con el estaré yo en la angustia
Lo libraré y le glorificaré
Lo saciaré de larga vida,
Y le mostraré mi salvación.

Because he has set his love upon
Me, therefore I will deliver him:
I will set him on high, because he
hath known My name. He shall call
upon Me, and I will answer him.
I will be with him in trouble, I will
deliver him and honor him.
With long life will I satisfy him,
And show him My salvation.
—*Psalms 91:14–16*

The musicians pack away their instruments, unplug the electric guitars, and turn off the microphones. The modest pews are empty, and a few hermanos mill around chatting, calling out greetings to one another, and putting coats on small children. Coins clink together in a felt pouch as two elders count the offering and record the amount in a small book.

Sunday school has just ended, and it's time to go home. Believers step out into the cool, bright morning, children in tow, and trudge up the wide dirt street of the barrio. Buses pass and cloud them with dust. Smells of fresh-baked bread and roasted chicken waft from the storefront shops. A middle-aged woman dumps a tub of laundry water into the dirt street from her second-story cement rooftop, startling two scrawny dogs below who were busy investigating a pile of garbage.

Though the believers' identity with the "world" was lost at conversion and baptism, they must continue living *in the world,* and church meetings must eventually come to a close. Their homes wait expectantly for them, and the responsibilities of children and work are pressing. Loads of laundry are soaking to be hand-washed and hung on clotheslines. Customers will arrive soon to their tiny shops to haggle and promise later payment. The youngest child has an earache, and his cry is piercing and anguished. A rat got into the food bin and died behind the potatoes; is the food okay?—because there is no money until Friday. The tenants upstairs were brawling last night and smashed a window, but it could be dangerous to mention it because the younger man is known for his violent temper. Community leaders are knocking door-to-door to collect money for a sewage pipe, but if the family contributes, there won't be any money to take the bus to work tomorrow.

Here is where the believers' faith is put to the test. It is easy to sing about trust and love and strength during the worship services, and "Amens" are never lacking when the pastors speak of commitment to God through the daily struggles. However, back at home, surrounded with urgent needs and grueling living conditions, where is God? How can the believers apply what they've learned in church to daily situations? How will they be able to trust God when the neighbors are murdered and the children's school fees double and the factory begins to lay off workers? How is the believers' faith maintained in daily life?

The focus of this study has come full circle. In early chapters, we explored how the situations of daily life are the initial motivation for many people to enter a Pentecostal church. Individuals in need seek out its immediate spiritual and practical solutions, its emotional support and miracle-making power. As the new converts become immersed in the Pentecostal worldview and frequent meetings, their motivation for church attendance is transformed into a desire for intimacy with the divine. Religious faith is strengthened through the stages of commitment, and the believers begin to devote much of their time and resources to the fervent mission of the church. As described in the previous chapter, frequent church meetings lift the believers' spirits and give them refreshing doses of hope, joy, and meaning. However, actual participation in the church only represents about 10 percent of the believers' waking hours. Their lives are still dominated by long bus commutes, household chores, taxing workdays, child rearing, barrio improvement, studies, and family activities. We have returned once again to daily life struggles.

If the believers' worldview is all-encompassing, and their profession of faith real, these convictions will manifest in daily life. The question is, How is the translation of faith between church environment and normal life accomplished?

This chapter will address the issue of faith maintenance in daily life. First I will explore the way in which believers make rational choices about their "daily walk with God." I will then examine the concept of worldview saturation in understanding how they make choices in difficult situations. Finally, stories and testimonies from the believers' own lives will be presented to illustrate their faith in action when confronted with common struggles of life in the barrio.

Choosing to Believe

Individual faith in biblical promises and in the reality of the divine is not a given fact in the life of a believer. After conversion, one does not enter into a fixed state of trust in the provision, protection, and care of God that can withstand any trial. The strength of one's faith cannot be assumed on the basis of verbal commitment. Nor is faith constant, for it fluctuates depending on daily actions and decisions. Believers continually choose whether they will act in accordance with the evangélico beliefs and practices in all of the events of life.

Surrounded with influences and lifestyles that are averse to the religious convictions of Pentecostalism, believers must consciously commit themselves to maintaining the faith. Each situation is a point of decision. Individual faith can be strengthened or weakened depending on the strategies of survival the believers choose to use. For example, the evangélica mother with a sick child may decide to fast and pray for healing, she may borrow money for medicine, or she may take the child to a service and ask the pastor for supernatural intervention. Each option will have a different effect on how she perceives divine power and resolution. Her decision will influence her faith, as will other situations, for individual faith is dynamic. It can soar after a miracle, and plummet during a crisis. The evangélicos make rational choices to believe based on their perception of what is the most plausible, effective strategy of action.

Does this mean that there is a constant grappling of possibilities in every situation, or that individual faith endures perpetual fluctuation? Certainly not. Many believers reach a steady state of devotion and faith. When problems arise, they act decisively and immediately because they have disciplined themselves to respond to situations with belief and action. These believers are making choices based on rationale determined long before any problem arose. This is called "strength of conviction," which develops through experience, training, and religious passion. As soon as the child shows suspicious symptoms, the mother drops to her knees and begins to pray for divine healing. The point of decision passed so quickly that it was almost unnoticeable.

Individual believers vary in the strength of their convictions, depending on what stage of maturity they have reached in the faith. Some of those in my study were new converts who had not yet been accustomed to acting in faith for their daily life circumstances. Others were longtime believers so grounded in their evangélico identity that the two were inseparable. The difference between these was found in one's biblical training and the degree of participation and commitment that had been maintained since conversion. It was also based on the intensity of the individual's religious worldview.

Worldview Saturation

Worldview adherence is the force that determines the believers' decisions in daily life situations. An individual totally saturated in the Pentecostal worldview acts, speaks, and lives in complete accordance with his or her church's teaching and spiritual leaders' examples. The individual whose worldview reflects both secular ideas and religious thought behaves and speaks with a mixed rationale. The degree to which a believer conforms to the ideals of the high-cost, high-commitment, strict, and radical Pentecostal faith determines the intensity of his or her worldview. This worldview in turn determines the rational choices the believer makes through the ongoing struggle of daily life.

The concepts of rational choice and worldview saturation aid in understanding the high commitment level of the believers in this study. First let us examine how the evangélicos saturate themselves with the faith in a constant effort to think and live in accordance with its beliefs.

Meeting God at Home

One bright Sunday morning in late April, I walked up the narrow dirt street to the main avenue of the barrio, past the open bread stores and the parked buses, around piles of garbage and playing children, and down another narrow street to Loida's house. She was making a big batch of tamales (a traditional Colombian food) for a family gathering, and had invited me to join her.

Loida's teenage daughter answered my knock, and as I entered, I could hear the sound of praying in the center patio by the kitchen. There was Loida and her mother Luisa, surrounded with large, flat banana leaves, steaming pots of chicken and vegetables, and a half-dozen finished tamales. They were standing with eyes closed, listening to the broadcast of a service from a large church in Bogotá. The preacher was recounting his conversion story, using slow words wrought with chilling emotion to describe how his life had been rescued by God's great forgiveness and love.

Audibly weeping, he began to lead the congregation and the radio audience in a fervent prayer of repentance and commitment to God. You could hear the dim roar of thousands of praying voices from the church congregation as the preacher urged, "Pray, hermanos. Cry out to God and give him the burdens of your heart." Loida and Luisa began to pray as fervently, eyes still closed, lifting their cornmeal-covered hands into the air. Tears were streaming down Loida's face, and she cried, *"Si, Señor, tú eres grande, límpiame con tu presencia esta mañana, Padre Santo, te exalto, te glorifico, Oh Dios lindo, si Señor . . ."*

Her mother, a tiny woman with long gray hair pulled into a clip behind her head, stood in the brightly lit patio, worshiping in a raised voice, oblivious to the world around her. Minutes later, the sermon ended, and the two women greeted me, smiling, wiping tears, and exclaiming, *"Qué bendición!"* (What a blessing!) We set to work making more tamales, and they bubbled over with praise for the anointing, or the charged spirituality, of the hermano's sermon.

Maintenance Activities

During my research, I made many frequent, unannounced visits to the homes of evangélicos in the barrio, which allowed me to see how deeply their faith was incorporated into daily living. Women would usually be doing *oficio* (household chores), vigorously scrubbing clothes against a cement wash basin, preparing food over the two-burner gas stoves, or scouring the cement floors with a broom and cold soapy water. They would immediately heat up some tinto and offer it to me with fresh bread. I would perch on a stool or wooden chair, keeping them company as they continued doing oficio, and we'd chat about the family, the church, the situation of the country, or the never-ending nuisance of thick mud in the streets. If they tended a small store from the front of their home, I'd accompany them, making conversation about how business had been or how the children were.

More often than not, the conversation would drift to serious issues and intimate concerns about the family, employment, recent accounts of violence or theft, and personal relations. The language they used always made reference to their faith in God: attributing difficulties to spiritual causes, praising God for good news, expressing the need to pray for a solution to a problem, or explaining biblical principles to make sense of any situation within the home, work, city, or world. Matthew 12:34 says, "Out of the abundance of the heart, the mouth speaks," and the believers' constant verbal expression of their faith evidenced its prominent role in their lives. They maintained its prominence through a number of home "maintenance" activities.

In many homes, I noticed that the believers kept a constant "evangelical environment" by imitating church practices throughout the day. Bogotá's Christian radio station was almost always on, filling the home or storefront with music from contemporary South American evangelical artists, broadcasted sermons, biblical teachings, and congregational worship. These gave the sense of actually being in a church, participating in divine presence and power. The description of Loida and Luisa that opened this section provided a good example of how broadcasted services can have a profound impact on evangélicos throughout the city. Diana, who stayed home with her three children, played worship cassettes and sang with them as she cleaned and cooked.

The stark cement or brick walls of most Pentecostal homes were decorated with Christian posters, Bible verses in painted ceramic, and twelve-month calendars with popular biblical passages. On a bookshelf one could find several used Bibles, perhaps a tambourine, and workbooks for biblical instruction. On my return trip to Nuevo Progreso, Ximena proudly showed me the splendid collection of Christian *cuadros* (wall hangings with verses and sayings) that she was saving for the completion of her family's new living space. Her intent, as she described to me, was to be ever conscious of the Lord and his purposes in her life.

The believers also engaged in prayer and Bible study on a regular basis. Eduardo worked fifteen- to eighteen-hour days in his own shoe repair shop in another barrio, yet he and his wife and four children prayed together every morning and night in their small living room. Diana led her children in a small *devocional* every evening, reading a chapter from the Bible and then praying in adoration and supplication to God. Marisol, who worked in a clothing factory in northern Bogotá, had to catch a bus at 4:30 A.M. to arrive at the factory before six o'clock. She set her alarm for 3:15 A.M. to have a half-hour of prayer as part of her preparation for the day. Alberto and his wife

Latiana would kneel in the darkness of the early morning to pray with their landlord, who was also an evangelical. "It's something wonderful to meet the Lord at that hour," Alberto told me, bouncing his baby son. "It's purer, because there are no distractions."

Many believers engaged in a constant discourse with God as events occurred throughout the day. They would pray about the weather, for an available bus, for the safety of their children, or for a successful workday. It was like an informal monologue, expressing gratitude for things that went well and supplication for the challenges. The believers were so confident in the unfailing presence of God with them in all of their labors that they would fall into prayer without needing any formal setting or special "link." Nothing was too small or too big to share with their closest confidant.

The evangélico emphasis on gaining biblical knowledge was also evident in the believers' daily lives. Churches often assigned the believers homework, such as reading several chapters of the Bible, filling out workbooks, memorizing verses, or learning church history and doctrine. Biblical study was a highly valued activity in all age groups of the congregation. It so permeated the purposes and goals of the churches that there was a noticeable appetite for knowledge of the Bible in the majority of church members. I can recall one sermon in which the pastor exhorted the hermanos to partake of the Bible many times a day, as spiritual food, in the same way that one has frequent meals. "Eat it for breakfast, eat it for lunch, have it for a snack, and then right before going to sleep. Read it day and night, and you will prosper," he preached.

When I first met Carlos in January 1996, he was a new believer. Due to his lack of education and poor reading skills, he viewed Bible study as a cumbersome activity. Nevertheless, Carlos enrolled in a leadership course in his church that required heavy Bible reading and workbook activity. Inspired by the extensive biblical knowledge of the pastor and church leaders, he determined to complete the course and learn enough to teach others about God.

A year after first meeting Carlos, I returned to the barrio and visited him. He was very pleased to tell me that he had risen to "level 3" of the courses offered by the church. When he discussed doctrine and biblical teachings with me, it was evident that he had learned a great deal. I also noticed crudely written Bible memory verses taped to the walls in several rooms of his small house. "There's no limit," he said enthusiastically of the church's Bible course. "You never graduate, because you can never stop learning." Carlos's individual desire to acquire a strong understanding of the Bible reflected that of many evangelicals in the barrio. Even the illiterate hermanos within the churches could recite important verses and lessons.

Fasting

Fasting was another common congregational activity that was practiced at home and work. It is taught in evangélico churches that if one goes without food in making a prayer, that petition gains special emphasis or favor before God. The believers also fast as a humility exercise before an important event to "increase the blessing." One may fast for successive half-days or full days. Common purposes of fasting are for church growth, spiritual cleansing, in support of pastors, in intercession for the salvation of an individual or of Colombia, or for special needs and emergencies.

Often, churches will have a *cadena de ayuno* or a fasting chain, in which different members are assigned to fast in their homes on successive days of the week. They believe that the outcome of a continuous fast is potent and effective:

> Esteban said that the fasting chain was to be done in the home, during whatever activity, and on Saturdays the entire church should be here fasting and praying. He explained that the thing about fasting is that you're denying food to your body, which is tremendous. He has a strenuous job carrying logs, and being in fasting with such work is tough. What's important is not necessarily that the believer be praying the entire day, but the fact that they're not eating, to support the pastor's ministry and for the restoration of the churches.
>
> —*Field Notes*

Julio fasted often for the conversion of his large family. When Diana faced economic hardship, she fasted for illumination from God about what she should do. Luisa's twin sons contracted meningitis as babies, and she fasted for two weeks for their healing. Alejandra sought a deeper holiness in her relationship with God, so she fasted and prayed regularly for successive half-days.

Fasting was a revered discipline among the evangelicals, because it forced them to deny the desires of the "flesh" and focus on the spiritual realm. It could be practiced within the daily routines of manual labor and domestic work, and didn't cost anything. The evangelicals considered it an essential part of prayer life to support the high goals of evangelization, spiritual cleanliness, and congregational strength that many churches had.

Home Meetings

Participation in home meetings was a standard practice for nearly all the evangelicals in this study. The churches designated a certain night every week for this activity and would divide their congregations into small groups or *celulas* (cells). These groups of believers would gather in homes across the city for a couple hours of intimate sharing, praying, worship, and informal Bible study, led by spiritual leaders in the church. Home meetings accomplished two main purposes for the churches.

First, it allowed believers to invite nonevangelical friends or relatives to a Pentecostal meeting without the formality of a normal church service. The members of the cell group could extend friendship and welcome to the visitors, attend to their personal needs through prayer and support, and still offer the gospel message in a nonthreatening way. In this way the home meetings were evangelistic, in keeping with the common goal of churches to proselytize entire barrios and win them to Christ.

The second, more central purpose to cell groups was to provide intimacy, accountability, and belonging to believers who attended larger churches. It is easy to lose the close sense of *compañerismo* in huge congregations where hundreds of people file in and out in an endless regimen of meetings. In the home meetings, believers knew one another by name and shared in the needs and struggles of everyone. Each person had an opportunity to give a testimony, lead prayer, direct a song, or even to be the "messenger of the Word" in edifying the other believers, giving a strong sense of personal worth in God's kingdom.

Within the home meetings existed a tiny network of resources, as believers were made aware of individuals' needs through prayer and sharing. In many ways, they were like miniature churches that served to encourage the believers midweek and offer spiritual "food" for the struggles of daily life that they all knew well. Since they were geographically based, individuals needed only to walk down a street or across the barrio to attend.

Loida and Abraham held a meeting in the front room of their home every Saturday evening, which I attended often. We would gather in a circle, using various types of seats and benches, and carry out many of the church practices in a more intimate manner. There was singing, praying, sharing of a Bible lesson, testimonies, and lots of close fellowship. Loida would then serve hot chocolate or coffee to all, with a piece of sweet bread. The believers who attended those meetings were as close as a family, deeply bonded by their consistent spiritual seeking and faith in God.

In sum, the Pentecostal believers engaged in fasting, prayer, Bible study, and home meetings on a regular basis during the week to maintain their faith and spiritual growth apart from church activities. In addition, the evangelicals consistently listened to Christian radio, saturating their minds with the teachings of the Pentecostal faith. By decorating their homes with inspirational Bible verses and Christian posters, they were constantly reminded of the purposes and goals of their lives as evangélicos in a "sinful world."

Committed believers in the barrio had a distinct, unmistakable environment within their home, demonstrating their conviction in the invisible kingdom of God. Although the church's ambiance was ideal, the believers aspired to also make their own abode a place for renewing encounters with God and spiritual training. Continually steeped in the worldview of the faith, they would be more apt to make decisions in accordance with it when confronted with the struggles of daily life.

This conscious, private effort to remain firm in the faith demonstrated the believers' sincere desire to follow God. If spiritual "holiness" were only a means to personal gain within the church, then the only manifestation of individual faith would be in weekly meetings. Yet their motivation was deeper, as Ximena expressed in her interview:

> I thank God, because he's with us every day. The Lord is most important in this world, over my husband, children, brother. And in the moment that he calls me, I want to be prepared. Not to fall away from the faith. We don't know the day he will call us. For me, I want to be in complete communion with the Lord every day, without failing him. His faithfulness is great. But to get closer to him every day, to give something more, not only what I have done, but every day, more.

In Times of Need

Stressful, disturbing situations of unemployment, sickness, economic need, and physical danger were frequent occurrences in the day-to-day life of families in Nuevo Progreso. In the long commute to northern Bogotá, where most residents were employed, buses often crashed or overturned. Passengers were packed so tightly, and the buses traveled at such velocity, jerking in their stop-and-go fashion, that one often was physically harmed during the two to four hours of daily travel to and from the city. As discussed in Chapter 2, Nuevo Progreso also had its share of crime, murder, and assault. There was very little safety and few rights for victims, causing deep distrust and hostility between residents.

The barrio was sanitarily unsafe as well, with untreated drinking water, open sewers, dirt streets, heaps of exposed garbage, and suspicious-smelling meat markets selling every imaginable animal part to the residents. Houses were not heated to combat the chilly nights, and the barrio streets were either whipped by dust and wind or covered in thick, sloppy mud and rushing streams. As a result, the children were especially plagued with sickness, and one's health was constantly in danger.

Most of the residents of the barrio could not afford to be sick, for it meant spending precious resources and jeopardizing their employment. They would take herbal remedies and continue in the wearisome schedule in spite of pain or hounding symptoms. Back pain, sprained muscles, and physical fatigue were simply endured as part of life.

Evangélico residents of Nuevo Progreso, although living in the same circumstances of poverty and danger, had a different outlook on the situations that threatened their well-being. They believed that God would supernaturally intervene on their behalf, either by direct divine care, congregational support, or provision from nonevangelical relatives and friends. However the solution was provided, the believers attributed its source to God and consequently grew in their faith that he was their sustainer. Many counteracted their difficult situations by entering into desperate supplication and fasting, and then rested in the confidence that God had heard their prayers and would respond favorably. When their spiritual food "intake" was high, their spirits were strong, and their decisions to act reflected the evangélico belief in total dependence on providential care.

In this section I examine three common situations of need and how the believers acted in each one with their faith. Experiences with "miracles" and "blessings" are great catalysts for individual faith. Faith renewal works in a self-perpetuating cycle: higher motivation produces stronger church participation, which saturates the believers in the Pentecostal worldview. This worldview determines their decisions to act in faith during difficult situations of daily life, and these decisions, once brought to fruition, increase the believers' motivation. In this section I will use the evangélicos' own stories to illustrate the relationship between their constant struggles and their faith.

Divine Provision

Due to Colombia's fragile economy and the low quality of jobs held by barrio residents, the families in my study often lacked food or money. Divine provision was the most celebrated supernatural occurrence, for economic need was a never-ending challenge. Many times, believers did not know from where money would come for upcoming bills or expenses. There would be food for a couple more days, but the paycheck was a week away. Hospital bills from medical emergencies such as serious illnesses or accidents reached sums higher than their annual income, which they could not fathom paying alone.

Education for the children was also very expensive, requiring a monthly pensión, uniforms, books, supplies, and sometimes transportation. Evangélicos with their own small businesses needed loans, merchandise, and money for overhead expenditures. The cost of living was so unstable, and expenses so unpredictable, that it was almost impossible for many families to plan their finances or budget their salaries. Economic need was an ever-present reality that threatened hunger and destitution to those without sources of support.

The believers displayed varying degrees of trust in the divine during these situations. In the interviews, I presented the evangélicos with a common economic dilemma and asked how they would resolve it. Three-fourths responded that they would first pray and entrust the situation to God, and he would provide food or money through people they knew or in a "supernatural" fashion. During my visits, I often witnessed how believers would maintain their faith in divine provision in spite of discouraging circumstances.

One Wednesday I went to visit Diana, who was feeling *desanimada* (discouraged). Her husband had begun working far away and wouldn't receive a salary for the first three months. Left with small children, Diana had pressing financial needs, and there was no money in sight:

> Went to see Diana. She had taken four buses to her husband's old work that morning to hear that there was no check. And she told them, "Please, I don't have a single peso." And still no. She felt rather depressed. She wasn't worried about food, because "God always supplies the food." For example, a neighbor had brought her a whole bunch of fruits and vegetables a couple of days before. It was the pensión—she would probably have to borrow money. But she said that she knew God would provide, and so she would wait on him. He knew her situation.
>
> —*Field Notes*

Moisés, a dark hermano from the coast of Colombia, had been seeking jobs for over two months without success. When asked how one should respond in these situations, Moisés explained the importance of faith to me:

If we leave something in God's hands, he will bless us. He is a merciful father. But you have to have an intense faith in God. Sometimes we ask and ask and the Lord doesn't give it to us. Our intellect begins to doubt God and we say, "It's not coming." But we need to have faith. It doesn't come because we are in doubt.

Since "*nada hay imposible para Dios*" ("there is nothing impossible for God," Luke 1:37), the evangelicals believe that divine provision may come through any channel—angels or atheists. They don't expect God to operate in any one form, but in various, unpredictable ways. Alejandra recounted such an experience:

> One time the Lord did a miracle in my life. My husband was without work, and I didn't have my little shop yet. Praying, I said, "Lord, I'm your daughter, and I don't have food, and you bless your children. Lord, you even touch the unbelievers to give." And I only prayed, I didn't tell anyone. And the Lord touched the heart of my brother-in-law, and he sent me 30,000 pesos for groceries. Then all the windows of heaven opened, because the next day my husband also found a job.

Rosalba, a beautician with her own little parlor in the barrio, had three school-age children. The morning of the interview, she fairly glowed with joy because of a recent "miracle." Her brother had leukemia, and he needed two months' wages to buy some medicine:

> We didn't have any money, and so yesterday I said, "Wait till next week, God will have the money for me, from work or from someone, I don't know." I was crying. Last night I cried. And this morning a friend arrived at the house to say hello to me. She said, "Rosalba, you told me that you needed money. I found some for you and I'm going to loan it to you." And she loaned me 100,000 pesos, so I could buy a part of the medicine. I'm very grateful to God. I just put it in his hands.

Olga, a mother of four, ran a small shop of miscellaneous clothing, school supplies, and candy from the front room of her home. Due to her husband's irregular employment and the fluctuating sales of her shop, there were times when she didn't have money for the family's food:

> I have been in these situations. On Tuesdays we buy the groceries. Sometimes there's no money for the food. So I say, "Okay, it's all

right, Lord, Thank you. You'll provide the food for next Tuesday."
That night, someone knocks on the door. "Look, here are groceries for you." I have seen the hand of the Lord in everything. I
know he loves me. If this happens, he sends something from
someplace, groceries.

Ximena passed through a time when the family income was one-
fourth the minimum wage. Her husband was building a little store for
her in front of a neighbor's house, and for almost a month her family
of four lived on the two days' wages Ximena received every week as a
maid in downtown Bogotá. She gave a testimony at a home meeting
during this time of how grateful she was for God's provision. She
echoed her faith in the interview:

> The Lord says in his word that he gives us our daily bread. I trust
> in this. Even if I don't have money for tomorrow, or food, I know
> that he's going to give it to me. The Lord has provided our needs.
> God has provided money, pensión for our son, all the food for
> the business. I've seen God there. God is wonderful. I was going
> to buy something, and I said, "God, you know I don't have the
> money." And an hermano loaned it to me.

The believers expressed faith in God's miraculous provision during short crises, and also in consistent long-term divine care. Josué,
an hermano in his late twenties, is a frail man who was born with several handicaps. During his childhood, his mother prohibited him
from any physical activity. Due to his limitations, his education was
minimal. Now as an adult, Josué has no manual strength or trained
skills to offer an employer. He lives alone, selling warm empanadas
from his doorstep or taking small jobs:

> I work for people who offer me jobs, who understand. I just can't
> do much! But it's a testimony because God provides for me. I
> always have food, a roof, a little money. I have the Father, the
> owner of all things. I save the money when I work, for when I
> need things. I've never lacked anything. I confess victory! The
> Lord is the only one who can help me.

Many evangelicals believed that God would not only provide for
daily bread and emergency situations, but also for better living conditions, higher salaries, cars, and other "blessings." As children of a
"king," they did not have to live begging, in destitute poverty, because
all of God's riches were available to them. I heard several pastors

preach that God wanted the best for his people, spiritually and materially. Believers like Alberto counted such provision among the testimonies of his life. Although only twenty, he had a wife and child and was already a leader in the church. He began work in construction (a common profession) at the age of thirteen and by his late teens had reached the esteemed level of a maestro. After the birth of his son, he bought a tiny piece of land in the barrio on which he would eventually construct his own home. After barely avoiding some legal scams that threatened to rob him of his land, Alberto was informed that if he didn't build soon, it would not be a valid piece of property and he would lose it. But at that time, he had no money or materials to do so:

> I began to use the Christian faith, praying, "Lord, free me!" I decided to talk to my boss. I said, "Don Ricardo, I have a little land but no money to build on it." He said, "What do you need?" I said, "I need sand, rocks, blocks, cement, barrels, money, everything!" And he looked at me and laughed, like I was asking much of him. But I knew that I went in the name of Jesus. So, looking at me he said, "All right. We'll do something. I can help you. I'm going to send you a free load of bricks, a free load of sand, blocks, everything, to your house, and I'm going to loan you money." I couldn't believe it! I'm so thankful, and amazed at how God works. I saw the hand of God in this. And I have seen the hand of God many times.

Reflecting the progressive goals of the barrio residents, many believers prayed for living improvements. These ranged from the small purchase of an alarm clock or blender up to a home or a business. The believers were taught in their churches that God would grant their desires, and all that they asked, believing, they would receive (Matthew 21:22). Carlos told me that he was asking God for the money to buy a taxi cab, since his motorcycle accident had caused him to lose his old job. Ximena was asking God for the time and resources to finish constructing the second story of her home. Diana told me that she was trusting God for a gas stove, since the electric one was useless during the frequent electricity outages. Newlyweds Paola and Elías were praying for money to open their own bread store. They only needed to have faith in God, and he would in turn provide for their needs and desires in miraculous ways.

The believers' stories may give the impression that events simply took place in their natural course as they would for any diligent, honest person. In many cases, perhaps this is so. But we must remember that the believers viewed all of life's situations and resolutions as having spiritual sources and divine purposes. Because their decisions in faith were based on a conviction in biblical principles, the outcomes of these decisions were also interpreted in the same light. Even the smallest pleasures in their daily lives were seen as coming from God, and the believers accepted no other explanation for their occurrence. What may seem to be coincidence or luck to the non-Pentecostal would be a fulfillment of scriptural promises for the evangélicos of Nuevo Progreso.

The Pentecostal worldview acquired during indoctrination was self-perpetuating in life situations, for it offered a meaning and solution to everything, relating it to God's higher purposes in his kingdom. Lack of food or abundance of food, danger or safety, violence or peace, high prices or bargains all found significance through church teachings and biblical doctrine. Therefore, simply by experiencing life, a committed believer could grow in his or her faith.

Divine Protection

Divine protection was the experience that occurred more to individuals than to families, and it was exclusive of church life or support networks. These were instances in which the believer's life or belongings were in danger, and by "sovereign intervention" he or she was able to escape unharmed or with possessions intact. Since death and violence are so imminent in the everyday lives of the barrio residents, the believers count dramatic events *and* daily survival among their "miracles." From my experience as a resident in the barrio, often in risky situations, I came to understand their gratefulness for life each new day.

The believers based their trust in God's protection on several key Bible verses. One of these is found in Psalm 91:11: "For he will command his angels concerning you to guard you in all your ways." Also Isaiah 54:17a: "No weapon formed against thee shall prosper." The latter was quoted during testimonies of those hermanos who escaped from being murdered or assaulted. They were confident that bombs, knives, guns, or any kind of weapon could not cause them any harm, out of the will of God.

The believers actively prayed every day and during dangerous situations that the blood of Jesus would cover them and protect them. It was symbolic protection that they believed was unparalleled in power. Believers would also command that in the name of Jesus, Satan's destructive forces of evil must flee and leave them in safety. In their view, this was as effective as the scores of bodyguards that top Colombian officials employed. Spiritually covered with Jesus' blood, they would travel, work, and carry on with home life, confident that miracles would have to occur before they could be touched by harm. Alejandra had a small "miscellaneous" shop in front of her home, and she had to take weekly trips to downtown Bogotá for merchandise:

> I went to supply the *miscelanea* in town, and three creepy men were going to rob me. So I prayed, "Blood of Jesus cover me. I'm not going alone, I go with the angels of heaven surrounding me." The men were following me. So the Lord led me to get on a bus, and nothing happened to me.

Elisabét is a nursery-school teacher in downtown Bogotá. For her first eighteen years of life, she was supported as a sponsor child by a couple in Canada. She is a firm believer in the demonic realm and in God's power:

> I have been in so many places where the people rob, attack, kill, and nothing has happened to me. Once it was a terrible accident. I was on a certain bus, but the Lord led me to get off. It crashed after that. Many people were injured and dead. I would have been dead, but the Lord guarded me.

Some believers maintain that even while under divine protection, they may experience accidents or life-threatening situations. They believe that such traumatic events permit God to demonstrate his healing power or miraculous intervention in spite of impossible odds. These accidents are counted among the miracles. Luisa, a veteran of the faith, told me this story:

> We were once caring for a pastor's children. The house was big, and the windows were open in the dining room and kitchen. I was in the kitchen. Then I felt an explosion. I felt something. My stomach was inflated. And I said, "In the name of Jesus Christ, I am healed, in the promises of God." I got down on my knees and began to pray. They looked at me, and I was bleeding here, and here, from where this bullet passed through my body. And *nothing*, nothing happened. They took an X ray, and the bullet hadn't touched a single organ or intestine. They never did take the bullet out of me. The Lord is my doctor.

Luisa's faith dominated every moment of her life. She was constantly praying and fasting, and spent hours in prayer every week for her six grown children and four grandchildren. Using the name of Jesus, she prayed for their salvation, their protection, and their daily needs. Luisa attested to the power of God by describing miracle after miracle that she had witnessed in her children.

Carlos worked in the city on his motorcycle, and sometimes he would take his wife, Marisol, and four-year-old son, Miguel Angel, to church or to do errands. Once he left the house alone with Miguel Angel, and they were both without helmets. Marisol recounted the event:

> Carlos and Miguel Angel left on the motorcycle, and they had a terrible accident. They should have been dead. But thanks to God, nothing happened to them. Nothing! Because I always ask God to care for them. To care especially for my son, because he's very important to me. Just imagine it, the motorcycle crashed and they were thrown over the entire car. They fell, one landed here and another there. It was terrible. Miguel Angel, so small and fragile, he would have died. But nothing happened, thanks to God.

Ana had been a maid in a large office building in downtown Bogotá for sixteen years. She had many stories of horrendous bus rides to and from the city in which her life was in clear danger. Once, in a small bus, the brakes failed while they were going down a long hill. "We picked up tremendous speed," she told me, "and everyone thought we were going to crash. I said, 'Thank you, Lord, because it is you that is driving this bus.'" The next moment the brakes returned, and everyone was safe. She recounted another similar story:

> A year ago, the bus I was in started racing with another bus, and when they began to brake, we thought we'd flip over the entire street. But I said, "Lord, I know that with you, nothing is going to happen to anyone." We crashed, and all the windows were broken. We had scratches, but everyone was okay. Various times the same thing has happened to me. These are miracles from the Lord. I go along with a tranquillity. I see the dangers but I have a confidence in God that nothing will happen to us.

Andrés, a cook, recalled a time when he went out drinking with some friends after his conversion and received a wake-up call:

> Sometimes your friends try to make you weak, to return to the ways of evil. So I let them take me. I accompanied my friends to

some place, and we drank some hard liquor. Afterward, I caught a taxi, and the men in the taxi attacked me. And they were going to kill me. I said, "Lord, forgive me. I know that this is happening because I'm returning to the world again." They threw a liquid into my eyes so I couldn't see, and then one said, "Let's kill him and toss him over there!" and I said, "Lord, help me!" The other guy said, "No, we already robbed him. Why do we want to kill him? What for?" and the other insisting and insisting. Finally, they threw me from the car, and I had a bad fall—it hurt my back. But I believe that one was with Satan, and God touched the other to save me. I arrived here, held my children, and said, "Thank you Lord that I'm alive." I know that it's because the Lord was with me in that moment.

The believers felt that God was with them at every moment of the day, never letting up his guard over their lives. They rested in the belief that God's presence was the greatest security available. María is a single mother of two young children who worked full time in a restaurant in downtown Bogotá. One morning when she left for work, her son was very sick. During the day, she begged the owner to let her go home and check on him. Finally he relented. When she returned to the restaurant later, she found blood and water everywhere. Two men had entered the restaurant and ordered the owner to put up his hands and get to the floor, fast. They thought that a strongbox of money was there and intended to steal it. Instead of obeying their orders, the owner dumped a large container of water over them, and they shot him five times and killed him. Several people were injured, and the restaurant was damaged by gunfire. María said to herself, "Thanks to God, he is protecting me." She described to me the peace she felt under God's protection:

Before leaving here I pray, and coming home I pray. I hear of things that were supposed to happen to me and didn't. Now, I'm happy. I'm not afraid to go out into the street. Before, at nine at night, it scared me to go out—because of attackers here and there. But I go out, *contenta*. I'm not afraid. It's like you have the Lord at your side, accompanying you and protecting you. I feel this when I go out, a peace. When I was in the world, I'd be thinking at every moment what might happen. Fear of everything. Now, no. You walk with God and you don't fear anything.

It is important to note that the believers did not have danger-free lives, nor did they always escape harm. Many of the female believers suffered physical and emotional abuse at the hands of their nonevangelical husbands at home. Carlos had a serious motorcycle accident several weeks after I left the barrio in which his lower leg folded completely in half. He was bedridden for a couple of months and was still in great pain upon my return visit. One believer told us how a gang of armed teenagers had entered the food store where she was shopping and robbed all of the customers and the store owner. The believers were not immune to violent death, either: Ana's husband was murdered before she moved into the barrio, and Roxana's husband, the pastor of a church, died in a construction accident when their youngest child was only a few months old.

The evangélicos did not assume that divine protection licensed foolish risks, nor did they believe that their life with God eliminated sudden death, personal tragedy, or violence. They believed in God's supernatural protection, but also held that God allowed certain trials so that the faith and trust of his children would grow. Therefore, safety and danger, immunity and assault were all part of God's will. Referring to a theme I mentioned earlier, every event or situation in their lives held some divine meaning, even if it seemed nonsensical or devastating in the crisis moment.

One Saturday afternoon, I was visiting Melisa, who had invited two nonevangelicals over for hot chocolate and bread. The brother of one had just died, and Melisa was explaining her own evangelical interpretation of the tragedy. She shared how her own father had died only two months before, and said, "You may think this is not the time to hear about God. But this may be the most important time to know about his love." Melisa acknowledged that sadness and traumatic situations happen to everyone, but that God is there like a rock to sustain and strengthen. Her short evangelistic talk reflected the shared belief of many evangélicos: life's difficulties and tragedies happen to believers and unbelievers both, but the best route is to cling to the faith that gives it all eternal meaning and divine purpose. The simple belief that all situations were under God's control made it easier to bear hardship or pain. "It's all for the good," they told me.

Faith Healing

Supernatural healing was a divine manifestation that held great importance in the daily lives of the believers. Personal health was a critical concern, for it determined the degree to which one could carry out the essential tasks of living. Without health, one could not work and earn money for food and bills. Without strength, basic household chores such as hand-washing clothes or scrubbing floors became impossible. Without vigor and energy, care for children or invalid relatives could be dangerously neglected.

Esperanza, a single mother of three young boys who worked sixty- to eighty-hour weeks in a private club in downtown Bogotá, said to me, "With my health I have everything. Without my health I have nothing." The only way that Esperanza could successfully manage her children, employment, and home was to maintain a high energy level of activity and work. Her need for sound health was shared through all the members of the barrio. In this light, the strong attraction to the evangélicos' belief in divine healing is understandable.

The believers held that God was the great healer and doctor for all his children, but that divine healing only occurred through the believers' faith in his power. Girded with this doctrine, the believers in my study refused to question God's ability to intercede in any cir- cumstance of illness, whether it be temporal or terminal. In the inter- views, I presented them with a common situation—a child is gravely ill, worsening, and there are no funds to buy the needed medicine. What would they do? Three-fourths of the respondents said that they would trust in God's healing power to make the child well or in God's divine provision to buy the medicine. Either way, it was up to God. The believers based their faith on shared testimonies and personal experiences of what they called God's healing power. Abraham responded to this question with zeal: "I would trust in the Lord, who is our healer. Asking him with all our faith and with all our heart, he heals and saves. And God is so great and powerful, if we ask him with faith, he saves us, heals us, and grants us our requests."

Maricel was an elderly hermana in the church who helped care for her widowed lady pastor. She cried often during the interview, recalling times of sadness or hardship in her life. Speaking earnestly about her close relationship with God, Maricel recalled a time that she experienced healing:

> I was with a Christian sister and I felt sick. I remembered that the brother said that sicknesses are from Satan. I began to pray there in the church and rebuke the sickness, with my arms open, pray- ing to God. But while I was praying, I saw the Lord, like you see in the Catholic Church. He was coming with long hair, with his arms open. And I felt a desire to cry, a joy. I kept praying, I saw him so sweet, so tender. And afterward I felt no sickness in me. The Lord took the sickness away from me. I have asked him a lot for my health. I say, "Lord, I don't want to go to the doctors. I don't have the money. You are the only *médico* that I have in my life." And he heals me. He takes all the sicknesses from my body.

The evangélicos based their belief in divine healing on several biblical passages. Loida often went to neighbors' homes to pray for their healing as a form of evangelism, and her favorite Bible passage for these visits was James 5:14: "Is any one of you sick? He should call the elders of the church to pray over him and anoint him with oil in the name of the Lord. And the prayer offered in faith will make the sick person well; the Lord will raise him up." Loida and her brothers and sisters were brought up in the practice of divine healing. They all recounted stories to me of their mother Luisa's refusal to take them to doctors when they were younger. Instead, she would fast, pray, and believe in "the name of Jesus" that they would be healed. I asked Luisa what she would do if her young grandson were sick, and before I could finish the question, she broke in with strong affirmations of faith:

> In God, nothing is impossible. In the name of Jesus, he's healed. Healed of the sickness. When Daniel was a little boy, a toddler, the Lord did a great work in him. He had a dangerous sickness, and for two weeks he was very grave. He looked more dead than alive. And I prayed, fasted, night and day. One day they were preaching on the radio, at 6 A.M. The preacher gave the message about Isaiah 53 [which claims that Jesus eliminated sickness in his crucifixion]. And this hermano was very anointed in the Holy Spirit. I sat next to my son, and closed my eyes. "In the name of Jesus this child is healed. God is going to respond to my cry." The brother finished the message and prayed that powerful prayer. And I opened my eyes and the boy was completely healed, smiling. The Lord has done many miracles in his life.

Divine healing took on dramatic emphasis during life-threatening illnesses such as that with Luisa's son. It also held practical purposes for the believers' daily work. Gloria told me, "I suffered from this hand—it wouldn't move anymore, like it was asleep. I told the hermana Roxana to anoint me with oil, and God took away the sleepiness. Now I can wash, I can do chores, Glory to God."

Just as in the Bible Jesus had healed individuals who had been afflicted by lifelong illnesses, the believers in the barrio also claimed "deliverance" from seemingly interminable sicknesses. One sunny afternoon, I sat with Ximena in her little store as she recounted the touchstones of her faith in God. There was one in particular for which she was grateful:

> My God is wonderful, so *maravilloso*. He's done so many things for me. There are so many people who need the Lord and just don't

realize what he can do for them. For example all my life I've had epileptic seizures. And I've always had to take pills for it, five or six a day. Once I prayed to the Lord, "My God, I don't want to take any more pills." I knew a healer, and in him all is possible. I stopped taking pills for a couple of days, and then started again. And I prayed, "God, I know you can heal me, please, I don't want to take the pills anymore." And I stopped taking them. Now, a year and a half has passed, and I am normal, healed, and haven't had any seizures. God healed me, and I am grateful.

No matter the source, nature, or length of the illness or affliction, the necessary source for divine healing always came back to individual faith in God's power to perform miracles.

As discussed in the previous chapter, the evangélicos witnessed acts of divine healing on a weekly basis in the church. They were taught to believe that God's power would be evident from the smallest case of the cold to hopeless, terminal illnesses such as cancer or internal diseases. Although the believers' use of doctors varied, they all shared a view of God's healing power that could surpass medical science and human understanding. They prayed for it, expected it, and then shared their experiences with other hermanos to stimulate faith and thanksgiving. In their everyday life struggles, divine healing played a practical and spiritual role, cementing the believers' conviction in the reality of their God.

Devotion

Through the chapters of this study, we have followed the progression of conversion, commitment, and ongoing devotion of individuals to the evangelical faith in Bogotá, Colombia. By using the believers' own words, stories, and lives, I have attempted to demonstrate the deeply personal nature of this faith. From indoctrination to spiritual experiences, from divine healing to worship, from water baptism to Christian radio, the evangelical religion permeates every aspect of an individual's life and draws him or her into new life purposes, a new identity, and a transformed worldview.

The sacrifices and changes demanded in commitment to the faith dissuade those who join for purely superficial or selfish interests. Of those who remain, many have an unshakable conviction that God is real, active, and deeply loving. This belief deepens and strengthens as a result of what the evangélicos perceive to be manifestations of God's presence in their daily lives. "Supernatural" experiences are "proof" for the believers that what they hold is the truth. Many demonstrate an amazing faith in God, making significant sacrifices of time, money, and energy to the cause of the faith with little visible compensation or "benefits."

Their motivation? Often I found no other explanation for such commitment than the believers' sincere passion for God. Their actions revealed it, and their words expressed it. Not every believer held this zeal, nor did all express similar desires about their faith in God. All experienced valleys and mountains in their faith, feeling discouraged at times and elated at others. However, under the daily struggle and the fluctuating motivation, there was usually a core of belief as unshakable as a rock. In the intimacy of the interviews, I witnessed a heartfelt zeal and emotion that often amazed me. Having experienced the difficult barrio life and witnessed untold struggles in many believers' lives, I knew that their faith had been shaken from every side. Yet they continued on, even when it was more practical to forgo their commitment. They believed that when everything else had failed them, God would be there.

The amount of data collected during the research allowed me to go in a number of directions with this study. As I studied the recurring themes, however, I could not overlook the religious passion that was expressed so frequently. Therefore, in closing, I feel it would be a disservice to the believers to omit what really captures the essence of their faith. I present here a couple of these descriptions, for they are the best illustration of this passion. Here is Diana:

> I can believe in God, and I am sure he exists, because I can see, through the days and each second that passes, that God exists. That's why I have faith. I believe that with the single fact that we live, we can have faith in him. With the single fact that we can feel the air, that today it rained. Because God has shown me his mercy, giving me healthy children, without defects. This helps my faith to grow, to become strong.
>
> He helps me because when it seems like the whole world is tumbling toward me, God is there like a rock. He makes me feel strong because I can see the miracles in my home, in my economic life. He knows the need of each one of us and has given me my daily bread. God is my strength, my refuge, my castle, in whom we can trust. We can see him in the daily passing of life. All the time we can see his presence, and that's why I thank him. Without him we would not live.

Angela's words opened Chapter 4 and will close this study:

The gospel is like a way of roses, very beautiful, on the left and on the right, and I have to penetrate and find a way. And these roses have thorns. Thorns that are big, sharp, they hurt you, cause you to bleed. Even though they scratch me, I need to keep going. To keep the peace and holiness, without which no one will see God. People want to see Jesus because of interest, because he heals, gives money and prosperity. No, I invite you to meet the King of Heavens. The first thing is to love the Lord. Everything else is extra. With all your heart, soul, mind, and strength. If I don't use all those, I fall. A Christian who thinks he's not going to suffer won't last. His faith will be founded on sand. It's worth the trouble to follow the Lord. He is the only one who can help us. *Without God, we are nothing.*

8

Postscript

From the outside, Latin American Pentecostalism seems to be fueled by the great economic, social, and political upheaval that has shaken the southern continent. Millions in the working class are disillusioned by endless hardship, fearful for the insecurity of life and hope, and desperate to find help for their pressing material needs. To the outsider, the evangélico churches appear to fill a great void in working-class lives, offering practical and social networks of support that work as life buoys in the storm of survival.

From the inside, this religious movement seems to draw its life from the intimate relationship that believers claim to enjoy with God. Their prayers, songs, testimonies, and daily behavior display a sincere devotion that cannot be explained simply by a calculation of costs and benefits. The believers' faith is their greatest passion, their reason for living, and their source of strength and hope. Their churches are not storehouses of resources for survival, but channels for the exchange between God and believer. Practical purposes are achieved within the congregational activities, but they are not the focus. The focus is knowing God and making him known to the "unsaved" world.

To overlook the deeply spiritual nature of Latin American Pentecostalism in academic study is to regard believers as puppets in a great macrostructural drama. Contrasting this common image is the revelation that this movement is fueled by the passion of the human heart. The zealous faith of each individual believer is like a tiny match that, combined with 60 million others, has created an enormous blaze, catching the attention of the world.

This study is an attempt to demonstrate this notion of spiritual intimacy, delving into the personal faith of working-class believers in Bogotá. With stories, descriptions, and careful analysis, I have tried to weave a written tapestry that begins with unbelief and ends with fervent devotion, so that the reader may lean back, gaze upon its entirety, and gain a more profound understanding of the movement and its palpable influence in Latin America. If this has been achieved even to a modest degree, then I am most gratified.

Yet even as I reflect on the insight gained through this study, I recognize that many facets of the Latin American Pentecostal movement remain undivulged. For example, what happens to individual faith if the believer moves out of poverty? How might the evangelical worldview and its growing influence impact the future of Colombia? How might the evangelical churches be mobilized to social action in pursuit of their goal to bring Colombia to Jesus? Why does personal faith die away, and what are the circumstances in which this happens? What becomes of those who convert to the faith and yet cannot commit? What are the dynamics within evangelical churches that damage personal faith? During my research, I caught passing glimpses into these issues, which inspire me to continue exploring the movement. My hope is that this study will be a source of motivation for those who share such interests.

Written language provides at best a tarnished view of what the observer sees and experiences amidst the Latin American Pentecostals. How does one describe the anguished and desperate tone when a believer is praying for salvation of a loved one? How is it possible to portray the passion of believers worshiping in spiritual tongues, oblivious to the world around them? What words can one choose to describe a faith that stands against impossible odds? I only hope that their passion, which impacted me so deeply, might find an echo in my own words, so that the reader might begin to understand the powerful impact of the movement in the hearts and lives of others, of dozens, of millions.

Bibliography

Alape, Arturo, 1995. *Cuidad Bolivar: La hoguera de las ilusiones.* Bogotá: Colombiana Editorial.

Balch, Robert W., and David Taylor, 1977. "Seekers and Saucers: The Role of the Cultic Milieu in Joining a UFO Cult." In James T. Richardson, ed., *Conversion Careers: In and Out of the New Religions.* Beverly Hills: Sage.

Barrett, David B., ed., 1982. *World Christian Encyclopedia.* New York: Oxford University Press.

Berg, Michael, and Pablo Pretiz, 1994. *Mensajeros de esperanza: Los Evangélicos.* Miami: Editorial Unit.

Berger, Peter, 1967. *The Sacred Canopy: Elements of a Sociological Theory of Religion.* New York: Doubleday.

Berryman, Phillip, 1995. "Is Latin America Turning Pluralist?" *Latin American Research Review* 30, no. 3: 107–122.

Brusco, Elizabeth E., 1995. *The Reformation of Machismo: Evangelical Conversion and Gender in Colombia.* Austin: University of Texas Press.

Bryant, M. Darrol, and Herbert W. Richardson, eds., 1978. *A Time for Consideration: A Scholarly Appraisal of the Unification Church.* New York: The Edwin Meller Press.

Burdick, John, 1993. "Struggling Against the Devil: Pentecostalism and Social Movements in Urban Brazil." In Virginia Garrard-Burnett and David Stoll, eds., *Rethinking Protestantism in Latin America.* Philadelphia: Temple University Press, pp. 20–44.

Clark, Walter Houston, 1958. *The Psychology of Religion.* New York: The Macmillan Co.

Coleman, John A., 1991. "Will Latin America Become Protestant?" *Commonweal* 118, no. 25: 59–63.

Collins, Randall, ed., 1983. *Sociological Theory.* San Francisco: Jossey-Bass Inc.

Cook, Guillermo, 1985. *The Expectation of the Poor: Latin American Base Ecclesiastical Communities in Protestant Perspective.* Maryknoll, NY: Orbis Books.

———, 1990. "The Evangelical Groundswell in Latin America." *The Christian Century* 107: 1172–1179.

———, 1994. "Protestant Presence and Social Change in Latin America: Constrasting Visions." In Daniel Miller, ed., *Coming of Age: Protestantism in*

Contemporary Latin America. Lanham, MD: University Press of America, pp. 119–141.

Cox, Harvey, 1995. *Fire from Heaven: The Rise of Pentecostal Spirituality and the Reshaping of Religion in the Twenty-First Century.* New York: Addison Wesley Publishing Co.

de Bucana, Juana B., 1995. *La Iglesia Evangélica en Colombia: Una historia.* St. Fe de Bogotá: Asociacion Pro-Cruzada Mundial.

Deiros, Pablo A., and Carlos Mraida, 1994. *Latinoamérica en Llamas: Historia y creencias del movimiento mas impresionante de todos los tiempos.* Miami: Editorial Caribe Inc.

DeMaria, Richard, 1978. "A Psycho-Social Analysis of Religious Conversion." In Darrol M. Bryant and Herbert W. Richardson, eds., *A Time For Consideration: A Scholarly Appraisal of the Unification Church.* New York: Meller Press, pp. 82–130.

Der Spiegel, 1991. "A Quiet Revolution in Latin America." *World Press Review* (March): pp. 30–31.

Durkheim, Emile, 1915. *The Elementary Forms of the Religious Life.* New York: The Free Press.

Escobar, J. Samuel, 1994. "The Promise and Precariousness of Latin American Protestantism." In Daniel Miller, ed., *Coming of Age: Protestantism in Contemporary Latin America.* Lanham, MD: University Press of America, pp. 3–35.

Fernandes, Rubem Cesar, 1992. *Censo Institucional Evangélico: CIN 1992, primeiros comentarios.* Rio de Janeiro: Nucleo de Pesquisa and Instituto de Estudos da Religiao (ISER).

Finke, Roger, and Rodney Stark, 1992. *The Churching of America 1776–1990: Winners and Losers in Our Religious Economy.* New Brunswick, NJ: Rutgers University Press.

Flora, Cornelia Butler, 1976. *Pentecostalism in Colombia: Baptism by Fire and Spirit.* Cranbury, NJ: Associated University Presses Inc.

Froehle, Bryan T., 1994. "Religious Competition, Community Building, and Democracy in Latin America: Grassroots Religious Organizations in Venezuela." *Sociology of Religion* 55, no. 2: 146–162.

Gabriel, L. H., 1994. *El bautismo en agua: Un baño inútil?* Bogotá: Centros de Literatura Cristiana.

Garrard-Burnett, Virginia, and David Stoll, eds., 1993. *Rethinking Protestantism in Latin America.* Philadelphia: Temple University Press.

Gerlach, Luther P., and Virginia Hine, 1968. "Five Factors Crucial to the Growth and Spread of a Modern Religious Movement." *Journal for the Scientific Study of Religion* 71: pp. 23–40.

———, 1970. *People, Power, Change: Movements of Social Transformation.* Indianapolis: Bobbs-Merrill Company Inc.

Gill, Leslie, 1990. "'Like a Veil to Cover Them': Women and the Pentecostal Movement in La Paz." *American Ethnologist* 17 (November): 708–721.

Glock, Charles Y., 1973. *Religion in Sociological Perspective: Essays in the Empirical Study of Religion.* Belmont, CA: Wadsworth Publishing Company Inc.

Goff, James, 1965. *Protestant Persecution in Colombia 1948–1958.* Cuernavaca, Mexico: CIDOC.

Goldin, Liliana R., and Brent Metz, 1991. "An Expression of Cultural Change: Invisible Converts to Protestantism Among Highland Guatemala Mayas." *Ethnology* 30, no. 4: 325–338.

Haddox, B.E., 1970. *A Sociological Study of the Institution of Religion in Colombia.* Ann Arbor, MI: University Microfilms.

Hanratty, Dennis M., and Sandra W. Meditz, 1990. *Colombia: A Country Study.* Washington, DC: Federal Research Division, Library of Congress.

Harrison, Michael, 1975. "The Maintenance of Enthusiasm: Involvement in a New Religious Movement." *Sociological Analysis* 36, no. 2: 150–160.

Heirich, Max, 1977. "Change of Heart: A Test of Some Widely Held Theories About Religious Conversion." *American Journal of Sociology* 83, no. 3: 653–680.

Helwege, Ann, 1995. "Poverty in Latin America: Back to the Abyss?" *Journal of InterAmerican Studies and World Affairs* 37 (Fall): 99–110.

Holy Bible. 1993. New International Version; *Santa Biblia,* 1960. Version Reina Valera (bilingual Bible) Nashville, TN: Holman Bible Publishers.

Houtart, Francois, and Emile Pin, 1965. *The Church and the Latin American Revolution.* New York: Sheed and Ward.

James, William, 1985. *The Varieties of Religious Experience.* Cambridge, MA: Harvard University Press.

Jeter, Hugo P., 1994. *Catolicismo Romano: Entendiendo a la Iglesia Católica Actual.* Barcelona: Editorial CLIE.

Kanagy, Conrad L., 1990. "The Formation and Development of a Protestant Conversion Movement Among the Highland Quichua of Ecuador." *Sociological Analysis* 50, no. 2: 205–217.

Kearney, Michael, 1984. *World View.* Novato, CA: Chandler & Sharp Publishers Inc.

Kelley, Dean, 1972. *Why Conservative Churches Are Growing: A Study in the Sociology of Religion.* New York: Harper & Row.

Lalive d'Epinay, Christian, 1969. *Haven of the Masses: A Study of the Pentecostal Movement in Chile.* London: Utterworth Press.

Lenkersdorf, Karl, 1971. "Revolution of the Roofless in Latin America." *Social Theory and Practice* 1, no. 31: 23–31.

Lindqvist, Sven, 1972. *The Shadow: Latin America Faces the Seventies.* New York: Books Inc.

Lofland, John, and Rodney Stark, 1973. "Becoming a World-Saver: A Theory of Conversion to a Deviant Perspective." In Charles Y. Glock, ed., *Religion in Sociological Perspective: Essays in the Empirical Study of Religion.* Belmont, CA: Wadsworth.

Luckmann, Thomas, 1967. *The Invisible Religion: The Problem of Religion in Modern Society.* London: The Macmillan Company.

Mackay, John A., 1932. *The Other Spanish Christ: A Study in the Spiritual History of Spain and South America.* New York: The Macmillan Company.

Mariz, Cecelia Loreto, 1994. *Coping with Poverty: Pentecostals and Christian Base Communities in Brazil.* Philadelphia: Temple University Press.

Martin, David, 1990. *Tongues of Fire: The Explosion of Protestantism in Latin America.* Oxford: Blackwell Publishers.

McGavran, Donald, 1963. *Church Growth in Mexico.* Grand Rapids, MI: William B. Eerdsman Publishing Co.

McGuire, Meredith B., 1977. "Testimony as a Commitment Mechanism in Catholic Pentecostal Prayer Groups." *Journal for the Scientific Study of Religion* 16, no. 2: 165–168.

Miller, Daniel, ed., 1994. *Coming of Age: Protestantism in Contemporary Latin America.* Lanham, MD: University Press of America.

Newell, William W., 1882. *Revivals: How and When?* New York: A. C. Armstrong and Son.

Nichol, John Thomas, 1966. *Pentecostalism.* New York: Harper & Row.

Poloma, Margaret M., and Brian F. Pendleton, 1989. "Religious Experiences, Evangelism, and Institutional Growth Within the Assemblies of God." *Journal for the Scientific Study of Religion* 28, no. 4: 415–431.

Read, William R., 1965. *New Patterns of Church Growth in Brazil.* Grand Rapids, MI: William B. Eerdsman Publishing Co.

Restivo, Sal, 1991. *The Sociological World View.* Cambridge, MA: Basil Blackwell Inc.

Richardson, James T., 1977. *Conversion Careers: In and Out of the New Religions.* Beverly Hills: Sage Publications.

Richardson, James T., and Mary Stewart, 1977. "Conversion Process Models and the Jesus Movement." In James T. Richardson, ed., *Conversion Careers: In and Out of the New Religions.* Beverly Hills: Sage.

Rosenburg, Tina, 1991. *Children of Cain: Violence and the Violent in Latin America.* New York: Penguin Books Inc.

Samuel, Vinay, and Chris Sugden, eds., 1983. *Sharing Jesus in the Two-Thirds World.* Grand Rapids, MI: William B. Eerdsman Publishing Co.

Saunders, George R., 1995. "The Crisis of Presence in Italian Pentecostal Conversion." *American Ethnologist* 22, no. 2: 324–340.

Schultze, Quentin J., 1994. "Orality and Power in Latin American Pentecostalism." In Daniel Miller, ed., *Coming of Age: Protestantism in Contemporary Latin America.* Lanham, MD: University Press of America, pp. 65–88.

Simmel, Georg, 1959. *Sociology of Religion.* New York: Philosophical Library.

Smith, Christian, 1994. "The Spirit and Democracy: Base Communities, Protestantism, and Democratization in Latin America." *Sociology of Religion* 55, no. 2: 119–143.

Snow, David A., and Richard Machalek, 1983. "The Convert as a Social Type." In Randall Collins, ed., *Sociological Theory.* San Francisco: Jossey-Bass Inc., pp. 259–289.

———, 1984. "The Sociology of Conversion." *Annual Review of Sociology* 10: 167–190.

Stack, Carol, 1974. *All Our Kin: Strategies for Survival in a Black Community.* New York: Harper & Row.

Steigenga, Timothy J., 1994. "Protestantism, the State, and Society in Guatemala." In Daniel Miller, ed., *Coming of Age: Protestantism in Contemporary Latin America.* Lanham, MD: University Press of America, pp. 143–172.

Stoll, David, 1990. *Is Latin America Turning Protestant? The Politics of Evangelical Growth.* Berkeley: University of California Press.

Stromberg, Peter G., 1990. "Ideological Language in the Transformation of Identity." *American Anthropology* 92 (March): 42–56.

Suchman, Mark C., 1992. "Analyzing the Determinants of Everyday Conversion." *Sociological Analysis* 53 (S): S15–S33.

Swatos, William H., Jr., 1994. "On Latin American Protestantism." *Sociology of Religion* 55, no. 2: 197–205.

Thornton, William Philip, 1981. "Protestantism: Profile and Process. A Case Study in Religious Change from Colombia, South America." Ph.D. Dissertation for Southern Methodist University.

Townsend, L.T., 1877. *The Supernatural Factor in Religious Revivals.* Boston: Lee and Shepard.

Turner, Ralph H., and Lewis M. Killian, 1957. *Collective Behavior.* Englewood Cliffs, NJ: Prentice Hall Inc.

Ullman, Chana, 1989. *Transformed Self: The Psychology of Religious Conversion.* New York: Plenum Press.

Weber, Max, 1963. *The Sociology of Religion.* Boston: Beacon Press.

Westmeier, Karl Wilhelm, 1986. "The Enthusiastic Protestants of Bogotá, Colombia: Reflections on the Growth of a Movement." *International Review,* January: 13–24.

Willems, Emilio, 1967. *Followers of the New Faith: Culture Change and the Rise of Protestantism in Brazil and Chile.* Nashville, TN: Vanderbilt University Press.

———, 1967. "Validation of Authority in Pentecostal Sects of Chile and Brazil." *Journal for the Scientific Study of Religion* 6: 253–258.

Wilson, Everet A., 1994. "The Dynamics of Latin American Pentecostalism." In Daniel Miller, ed., *Coming of Age: Protestantism in Contemporary Latin America.* Lanham, MD : University Press of America, pp. 89–116.

Wilson, John, and Harvey K. Clow, 1981. "Themes of Power and Control in a Pentecostal Assembly." *Journal for the Scientific Study of Religion* 20, no. 3: 241–250.

Yinger, J. Milton, 1946. *Religion in the Struggle for Power: A Study in the Sociology of Religion.* Durham, NC: Duke University Press.

Index

About the Book

Faith in the Barrios offers a rich and powerful perspective on evangelicalism in the barrios of Latin America, exploring conversion and subsequent commitments to faith in an unstable environment of poverty and violence.

Bomann's study, based on extensive fieldwork, is unique in that it reveals the evangelical Protestant movement through the eyes of the believers themselves, as well as from the author's combined religious and scholarly perspectives. Uncovering deep intimacies of devotion and struggle in the lives of residents of a marginalized neighborhood in Bogotá, Colombia, Bomann provides vivid description and careful analysis of a religious movement that is having a profound influence in Latin America.

Rebecca Pierce Bomann is a student of sociology and a practicing evangelical. This study was undertaken with the support of Hamilton College.